PENGUIN BOOKS — GREAT IDEAS

The Freedom to be Free

T0322141

Hannah Arendt

1906–75

Hannah Arendt
The Freedom to be Free

PENGUIN BOOKS — GREAT IDEAS

PENGUIN BOOKS

UK | USA | Canada | Ireland | Australia
India | New Zealand | South Africa

Penguin Books is part of the Penguin Random House group
of companies whose addresses can be found at
global.penguinrandomhouse.com.

These essays have been taken from
Thinking without a Banister, first published
in 2018 by Shocken Books, a division of
Penguin Random House LLC, New York.

This selection published in Penguin Books 2020
005

Set in 12/15 pt Dante MT Std
Typeset by Jouve (UK), Milton Keynes
Printed and bound in Great Britain by Clays Ltd, Elcograf S.p.A.

A CIP catalogue record for this book
is available from the British Library

ISBN: 978–0–241–47288–0

www.greenpenguin.co.uk

Contents

Contents

Labor, Work, Action

For this short hour, I should like to raise an apparently odd question. My question is: What does an active life consist of? What do we do when we are active? In asking this question, I shall assume that the age-old distinction between two ways of life, between a *vita contemplativa* and a *vita activa,* which we encounter in our tradition of philosophical and religious thought up to the threshold of the modern age, is valid, and that when we speak of contemplation and action we speak not only of certain human faculties but of two distinct ways of life. Surely, the question is of some relevance. For even if we don't contest the traditional assumption that contemplation is of a higher order than action, or that all action actually is but a means whose true end is contemplation, we can't doubt – and no one ever doubted – that it is quite possible for human beings to go through life without ever indulging in contemplation, while, on the other hand, no man can remain in the contemplative state throughout his whole life. Active life, in other words, is not only what most men are engaged in but even what no man can escape altogether. For it is in the nature of the human condition that contemplation remains dependent upon all sorts of activities – it depends upon labor to produce whatever is necessary to keep the human organism alive, it depends upon work to create whatever is needed to house the human body, and it needs action in order to organize the living together of many human beings in such a way that peace, the condition for the quiet of contemplation, is assured.

Since I started with our tradition, I just described the three chief articulations of active life in a traditional way, that is, as serving the ends of contemplation. It is only natural that active life has always been described by those who themselves followed the contemplative way of life. Hence, the *vita activa* was always defined from the viewpoint of contemplation; compared with the absolute quiet of contemplation, all sorts of human activity appeared to be similar insofar as they were characterized by un-quiet, by something negative, by *a-skholia* or by *nec-octium*, nonleisure or absence of the conditions which make contemplation possible. Compared with this quietude, all distinctions and articulations within the *vita activa* disappear. Seen from the viewpoint of contemplation, it does not matter what disturbs the necessary quiet as long as it is disturbed.

Traditionally therefore the *vita activa* received its meaning from the *vita contemplativa;* a very restricted dignity was bestowed upon it because it served the needs and wants of contemplation in a living body. Christianity with its belief in a hereafter, whose joys announce themselves in the delights of contemplation, conferred a religious sanction upon the abasement of the *vita activa* while, on the other hand, the command to love your neighbor acted as a counterweight against this sanction unknown to antiquity. Yet the determination of the order itself, according to which contemplation was the highest of the human faculties, was Greek, not Christian in origin; it coincided with the discovery of contemplation as the philosopher's way of life, which as such was found superior to the political way of life of the citizen of the polis. The point of the matter, which I can only mention here in passing, is that Christianity, contrary to what has frequently been assumed, did not elevate active life to a higher position, did not save it from its being derivative, and did not, at least not theoretically, look upon it as something that has its meaning and end within itself. And a change in this hierarchical order was indeed impossible so long as truth was the one comprehensive principle to establish an order among the human faculties, a truth moreover, which was understood as revelation, as something essentially given to man, as distinguished from truth being either the result of some mental activity – thought or reasoning – or as that knowledge which I acquire through making.

Hence, the question arises: Why was the *vita activa*, with all its distinction and articulations, not discovered after the modern break with tradition and the eventual reversal of its hierarchical order, the 'revaluation of all values', through Marx and Nietzsche? And the answer, though in actual analysis quite complicated, may be summed up briefly here: it is the very nature of the famed turning upside-down of philosophic systems or hierarchies of values that the conceptual framework itself is left intact. This is especially true for Marx who was convinced that turning Hegel upside down was enough to find the truth – i.e., the truth of the Hegelian system, which is the discovery of the dialectical nature of history.

Let me shortly explain how this identity shows itself in our context. When I enumerated the chief human activities: Labor-Work-Action, it was obvious that action occupied the highest position. Insofar as action related to the political sphere of human life, this estimation agrees with the pre-philosophic, pre-Platonic current opinion of Greek polis life. The introduction of contemplation as the highest point of the hierarchy had the result that this order was in fact rearranged, though not always in explicit theory. (Lip service to the old hierarchy was frequently paid when it had already been reserved in the actual teaching of the philosophers.) Seen from the viewpoint of contemplation, the highest activity was not action but work; the rise of the activity of the craftsman in the scale of estimations makes its first dramatic appearance in Plato's dialogues. Labor, to be sure, remained at the bottom, but political activity as something necessary for the life of contemplation was now recognized only to the extent that it could be pursued in the same way as the activity of the craftsman. Only if seen in the image of work, could political action be trusted to produce lasting results. And such lasting results meant peace, the peace needed for contemplation: No change.

If you now look upon the reversal in the modern age, you are immediately aware that its most important feature in this respect is its glorification of labor, surely the last thing any member of one of the classical communities, be it Rome or Greece, would have thought of as worthy of this position.

However, the moment you go deeper into this matter you will see that not labor as such occupied this position (Adam Smith, Locke, Marx are unanimous in their contempt for menial tasks, unskilled labor which helps only to consume), but *productive* labor. Again the standard of lasting results is the actual yardstick. Thus Marx, surely the greatest of the labor philosophers, was constantly trying to reinterpret labor in the image of the working activity – again at the expense of political activity. To be sure, things had changed. Political activity was no longer seen as the laying down of immutable laws which would *make* a commonwealth, having as its end result a reliable product that looked exactly as if it had originated in a blueprint by the maker – as though laws or constitutions were things of the same nature as the table fabricated by the carpenter according to a blueprint he had in mind before he began to make it. Political activity was now supposed to 'make history' – a phrase that occurred for the first time in Vico – and not a commonwealth, and this history, as we all know, had for its end product the classless society, which would be the end of the historical process just as the table is indeed the end of the fabrication process. In other words, since on the theoretical level no more was done by the great revaluators of the old values than to turn things upside-down, the old hierarchy within the *vita activa* was hardly disturbed; the old modes of thinking prevailed, and the only relevant distinction between the new and the old was that this order, whose origin and meaningfulness lay in the actual experience of contemplation, became highly questionable. For the actual event which characterizes the modern age in this respect was that contemplation itself had become meaningless.

With this event we shall not deal here. Instead, accepting the oldest, pre-philosophical hierarchy, I propose to look into these activities themselves. And the first thing of which you might have become aware by now is my distinction between labor and work which probably sounded somewhat unusual to you. I draw it from a rather casual remark in Locke who speaks of 'the labor of our body and the work of our hands.' (Laborers, in Aristotelian language, are those who 'with their bodies administer to the needs of life.') The phenomenal evidence in favor of this distinction is too striking to be ignored, and yet it is a fact that, apart from a few scattered remarks and important testimony of social and institutional history, there is hardly anything to support it.

Against this scarcity of evidence stands the simple obstinate fact that every European language, ancient or modern, contains two etymologically unrelated words for what we have come to think of as the same activity. Thus, the Greek distinguished between *ponein* and *ergazesthai*, the Latin between *laborare* and *facere* or *fabricari*, the French between *travailler* and *ouvrer*, the German between *arbeiten* and *werken*. In all these cases, the equivalents for labor have an unequivocal connotation of bodily experiences, of toil and trouble, and in most cases they are significantly also used for the pangs of birth. The last to use this original connection was Marx, who defined labor as the 'reproduction of individual life' and begetting, the production of 'foreign life', as the production of the species.

If we leave aside all theories, especially the modern labor theories after Marx, and follow solely the etymological and historical evidence, it is obvious that labor is an activity which corresponds to the biological processes of the body, that it is, as the young Marx said, the metabolism between man and nature, or the human mode of this metabolism which we share with all living organisms. By laboring, men produce the vital necessities that must be fed into the life process of the human body. And since this life process, though it leads us from birth to death in a rectilinear progress of decay, is in itself circular, the laboring activity itself must follow the cycle of life, the circular movement of our bodily functions, which means that the laboring activity never comes to an end as long as life lasts; it is endlessly repetitive. Unlike working, whose end has come when the object is finished, ready to be added to the common world of things and objects, laboring always moves in the same circle prescribed by the living organisms, and the end of its toil and trouble comes only with the end, i.e., the death of the individual organism.

Labor, in other words, produces consumer goods, and laboring and consuming are but two stages of the ever-recurring cycle of biological life. These two stages of the life process follow each other so closely that they almost constitute one and the same movement, which is hardly ended when it must be started all over again. Labor, unlike all other human activities, stands under the sign of necessity, the 'necessity of subsisting' as Locke used to say, or the 'eternal necessity imposed by nature' in the words of Marx. Hence, the actual goal of the revolution in Marx is not merely the emancipation of the laboring or working classes, but the emancipation of man from labor. For 'the realm of freedom begins only where labor determined through want' and the immediacy of 'physical needs' ends. And this emancipation, as we know now, to the extent that it is possible at all, occurs not by political emancipation – the equality of all classes of the citizenry – but through technology. I said: To the extent that it is possible, and I meant by this qualification that consumption, as a stage of the cyclical movement of the living organism is in a way also laborious.

Goods for consumption, the immediate result of the laboring process, are the least durable of tangible things. They are, as Locke pointed out, 'of short duration, such as – if they are not consumed – will decay and perish by themselves.' After a brief stay in the world, they return into the natural process that yielded them either through absorption into the life process of the human animal or through decay; in their man-made forms they disappear more quickly than any other parts of the world. They are the least worldly and, at the same time, the most natural and the most necessary of all things. Although they are man-made, they come and go, are produced and consumed, in accordance with the ever-recurrent cyclical movement of nature. Hence, they cannot be 'heaped up' and 'stored away', as would have been necessary if they were to serve Locke's main purpose, to establish the validity of private property on the rights men have to their own body.

But while labor in the sense of producing anything lasting – something outlasting the activity itself and even the life span of the producer – is quite 'unproductive' and futile, it is highly productive in another sense. Man's labor power is such that he produces more consumer goods than is necessary for the survival of himself and his family. This, as it were, natural abundance of the laboring process has enabled men to enslave or exploit their fellow men, thus liberating themselves from life's burden; and while this liberation of the few has always been achieved through the use of force by a ruling class, it would never have been possible without this inherent fertility of human labor itself. Yet even this specifically human 'productivity' is part and parcel of nature, it partakes of this superabundance we see everywhere in nature's household. It is but another mode of 'Be ye fruitful and multiply' in which it is as if nature herself speaks to us.

Since labor corresponds to the condition of life itself, it partakes not only in life's toil and trouble but also in the sheer bliss with which we can experience our being alive. The 'blessing or the joy of labor', which plays so great a part in modern labor theories, is no empty notion. Man, the author of the human artifice, which we call the world in distinction to nature, and men, who are always involved with each other through action and speech, are by no means merely natural beings. But insofar as we, too, are just living creatures, laboring is the only way we can also remain and swing contentedly in nature's pre-scribed cycle, toiling and resting, laboring and consuming, with the same happy and purposeless regularity with which day and night, life and death follow each other. The reward of labor, though it does not leave anything behind itself, is even more real, less futile than any other form of happiness. It lies in nature's fertility, in the quiet confidence that he who in 'toil and trouble' has done his part of nature in the future of his children and his children's children. The Old Testament, which, unlike clas-sical antiquity, held life to be sacred and therefore neither death nor labor to be an evil (certainly not an argument against life), shows in the stories of the patriarchs how unconcerned about death they were and how death came to them in the familiar shape of night and quiet and eternal rest 'in a good old age and full of years'.

The blessing of life as a whole, inherent in labor, can never be found in work and should not be mis-taken for the inevitably brief spell of joy that follows accomplishment and attends achievement. The blessing of labor is that effort and gratification follow each other as closely as producing and consuming, so that happiness is a concomitant of the process itself. There is no lasting happiness and contentment for human beings outside the prescribed cycle of painful exhaustion and pleasurable regeneration. Whatever throws this cycle out of balance – misery where exhaustion is followed by wretchedness or, on the other hand, an entirely effortless life in which boredom takes the place of exhaustion and the mills of necessity, of consumption and digestion, grind an impotent human body mercilessly to death – ruins the elemental happiness that comes from being alive. An element of laboring is present in all human activities, even the highest, insofar as they are undertaken as 'routine' jobs by which we make our living and keep ourselves alive. Their very repetitiveness, which more often than not we feel to be a burden that exhausts us, is what provides that minimum of animal contentment for which the great and meaningful spells of joy that are rare and never last, can never substitute, and without which the longer lasting though equally rare spells of real grief and sorrow could hardly be borne.

The work of our hands, as distinguished from the labor of our bodies, fabricates the sheer unending variety of things whose sum total constitutes the human artifice, the world we live in. They are not consumer goods but use-objects, and their proper use does not cause them to disappear. They give the world the stability and solidity without which it could not be relied upon to house the unstable and mortal creature that is man.

To be sure, the durability of the world of things is not absolute; we do not consume use-things but use them up, and if we don't, they will simply deteriorate, return into the overall process from which they were drawn and against which they were erected by us. If left to itself or expelled from the human world, the chair will again become wood, and the wood will decay and return to the soil from which the tree sprang before it was cut down to become the material with which men work and build. However, while usage is bound to use up these objects, this end is not planned before, it was not the goal for which it was made, as the 'destruction' or immediate consumption of bread is its inherent end; what usage wears out is durability. In other words, destruction, though unavoidable, is incidental to use but inherent in consumption. What distinguishes the most flimsy pair of shoes from mere consumer goods is that they do not spoil if I don't wear them, they are objects and therefore possess a certain 'objective' independence of their own, however modest. Used or unused they will remain in the world for a certain while unless they are wantonly destroyed.

It is this durability that gives the things of the world their relative independence from the men who produced and use them, their 'objectivity' that makes them withstand, 'stand against' and endure at least for a time the voracious needs and wants of their living users. From this viewpoint the things of the world have the function of stabilizing human life, and their objectivity lies in the fact that men, their ever-changing nature notwithstanding, can retrieve their identity by being related to the enduring sameness of objects, the same chair today and tomorrow, the same house, at least formerly, from birth to death. Against the subjectivity of men stands the objectivity of the man-made artifice, not the indifference of nature. Only because we have erected a world of objects from what nature gives us and have built this artificial environment into nature, thus also protecting us from her, can we look upon nature as something 'objective'. Without a world between men and nature, there would be eternal movement, but no objectivity.

Durability and objectivity are the result of fabrication, the work of *homo faber*. It consists of reification. Solidify, inherent in even the most fragile things, comes ultimately from matter which is transformed into material. Material is already a product of human hands that have removed it from its natural location, either killing a life process, as in the case of the tree which provides wood, or interrupting one of nature's slower processes, as in the case of iron, stone, or marble torn out of the womb of the earth. This element of violation and violence is present in all fabrication, and man as the creator of the human artifice has always been a destroyer of nature. The experience of this violence is the most elemental experience of human strength, and by the same token the very opposite of the painful, exhausting effort experienced in sheer labor. This is no longer the earning of one's bread 'in the sweat of his brow', in which man may indeed be the lord and master of all living creatures but still remains the servant of nature, his own natural needs, and of the earth. *Homo faber* becomes lord and master of nature herself insofar as he violates and partly destroys what was given to him.

The process of making is itself entirely determined by the categories of means and end. The fabricated thing is as end product in the twofold sense that the production process comes to an end in it and that it is only a means to produce this end. Unlike the laboring activity, where labor and consumption are only two stages of an identical process – the life of the individual or of society – fabrication and usage are two altogether different processes. The end of the fabrication process has come when the thing is finished, and this process need not be replaced. The impulse toward repetition comes from the craftsman's need to earn his means of subsistence, that is, from the element of labor inherent in his work. It also may come from the demand for multiplication on the market. In either case, the process is repeated for reasons outside itself, unlike the compulsory repetition inherent in laboring, where one must eat in order to labor and must labor in order to eat. Multiplication should not be confused with repetition, although it may be felt by the individual craftsman as mere repetition which a machine can better and more productively achieve. Multiplication actually multiplies things, whereas repetition merely follows the recurrent cycle of life in which its products disappear almost as fast as they have appeared.

To have a definite beginning and a definite predictable end is the mark of fabrication, which through this characteristic alone distinguishes itself from all other human activities. Labor, caught in the cyclical movement of the biological process, has neither a beginning nor an end properly speaking – only pauses, intervals between exhaustion and regeneration. Action, though it may have a definite beginning, never, as we shall see, has a predictable end. This great reliability of work is reflected in that the fabrication process, unlike action, is not irreversible:

every thing produced by human hands can be destroyed by them, and no use-object is so urgently needed in the life process that its maker cannot survive and afford its destruction. Man, the fabricator of the human artifice, his own world, is indeed a lord and master, not only because he has set himself up as the master of all nature, but because he is master of himself and his doings. This is true neither of laboring, where men remain subject to the necessity of their life, nor of acting, where they remain in dependence upon their fellow men. Alone with his image of the future product, *homo faber* is free to produce, and facing alone the work of his hands, he is free to destroy.

I said before that all fabrication processes are determined by the category of means and end. This shows itself most clearly in the enormous role which tools and instruments play in it. From the standpoint of *homo faber*, man is indeed, as Benjamin Franklin said, a 'tool-maker'. To be sure, tools and implements are also used in the laboring process, as every housewife proudly owning all the gadgets of a modern kitchen knows; but these implements have a different character and function when used for laboring; they serve to lighten the burden by mechanizing the labor of the laborer. They are, as it were, anthropocentric, whereas the tools of fabrication are designed and invented for the fabrication of things, their fitness and precision dictated by 'objective' aims rather than subjective needs and wants. Moreover, every fabrication process produces things that last considerably longer than the process which brought them into existence, whereas in the laboring process, bringing forth these goods of 'short duration', the tools and instruments it uses are the only things which survive the laboring process itself. They are useful for labor, and as such not the result of the laboring activity itself. What dominates laboring with one's body and incidentally all work processes performed in the mode of laboring, is neither the purposeful effort nor the product itself, but the motion of the process and rhythm it imposes upon the laborers. Labor's implements are drawn into this rhythm where body and tool swing in the same repetitive movement – until in the use of machines, it is no longer the body's movement that determines the movement of the implement, but the machine's movement that enforces the movements of the body, and which in a more advanced state, replaces it altogether. It seems to me highly characteristic that the much-discussed question of whether man should be 'adjusted' to the machine or the machines should be adjusted to the nature of man never arose with respect to mere tools or instruments. And the reason is that all tools of workmanship remain the servants of the hand, whereas machines demand that the laborer should serve them, adjust the natural rhythm of his body to their mechanical movement. In other words, even the most refined tool remains a servant unable to guide or to replace the hand; even the most primitive machine guides and ideally replaces the body's labor.

The most fundamental experience we have with instrumentality arises out of the fabrication process. Here it is indeed true that the end justifies the means; it does more, it produces and organizes them. The end justifies the violence done to nature to win the material, as the wood justifies killing the tree, and the table justifies destroying the wood. In the same way, the end product organizes the work process itself, decides about the needed specialists, the measure of cooperation, the number of assistants and cooperators. Hence, everything and everybody is judged here in terms of suitability and usefulness for the desired end product, and nothing else.

Strangely enough, the validity of the means-end category is not exhausted with the finished product for which everything and everybody becomes a means. Though the object is an end with respect to the means by which it was produced and the actual end of the making process, it never becomes, so to speak, an end in itself, at least not as long as it remains an object for use. It immediately takes its place in another means-end chain by virtue of its very usefulness; as a mere use-object it becomes a means for, let us say, comfortable living, or as an exchange object, that is, insofar as a definite value has been bestowed upon the material used for fabrication it becomes a means for obtaining other objects. In other words, in a strictly utilitarian world, all ends are bound to be of short duration; they are transformed into means for some further ends. Once the end is attained, it ceases to be an end, it becomes an object among objects which at any moment can be transformed into means to pursue further ends. The perplexity of utilitarianism, the philosophy, as it were, of *homo faber*, is that it gets caught in the unending chain of means and ends without ever arriving at some principle which could justify the category, that is, the utility itself.

The usual way out of this dilemma is to make the user, man himself, the ultimate end to stop the unending chain of end and means. That man is an end in himself and should never be used as a means to pursue other ends, no matter how elevated these might be, is well known to us from the moral philosophy of Kant, and there is no doubt that Kant wanted first of all to relegate the means-end category and its philosophy of utilitarianism to its proper place and prevent it from ruling the relations between man and man instead of the relationship between men and things. However, even Kant's intrinsically paradoxical formula fails to solve the perplexities of *homo faber*. By elevating man the user into the position of an ultimate end, he degrades even more forcefully all other 'ends' to mere means. If man the user is the highest end, 'the measure of all things', then not only nature, treated by fabrication as the almost 'worthless material' upon which to work and to bestow 'value' (as Locke said), but the valuable things themselves have become mere means, losing thereby their own intrinsic worth. Or to put it another way, the most worldly of all activities loses its original objective meaning, it becomes a means to fulfil subjective needs; in and by itself, it is no longer meaningful, no matter how useful it may be.

From the viewpoint of fabrication the finished product is as much an end in itself, an independent durable entity with an existence of its own, as man is an end in himself in Kant's moral philosophy. Of course, the issue at stake here is not instrumentality as such, the use of means to achieve an end, but rather the generalization of the fabrication experience in which usefulness and utility are established as the ultimate standards for the world as well as for the life of acting men moving in it. *Homo faber*, we can say, has transgressed the limits of his activity when, under the guise of utilitarianism, he proposes that instrumentality rule the realm of the finished world as exclusively as it rules the activity through which all things contained in it come into being. This generalization will always be the specific temptation of *homo faber* although, in the final analysis, it will be his own undoing: he will be left with meaninglessness in the midst of usefulness; utilitarianism never can find the answer to the question Lessing once put to utilitarian philosophers of his time: 'And what, if you please, is the use of use?'

In the sphere of fabrication itself, there is only one kind of object to which the unending chain of means and ends does not apply, and this is the work of art, the most useless and, at the same time, the most durable thing human hands can produce. Its very characteristic is its remoteness from the whole context of ordinary usage, so that in case a former object, say a piece of furniture of a bygone age, is considered by a later generation to be a 'masterpiece', it is put into a museum and thus carefully removed from any possible usage. Just as the purpose of a chair is actualized when it is sat upon, the inherent purpose of a work of art – whether the artist knows it or not, whether the purpose is achieved or not – is to attain permanence throughout the ages. Nowhere does the sheer durability of the man-made world appear in such purity and clarity, nowhere else therefore does this thing-world reveal itself so spectacularly as the non-mortal home for mortal beings. And though the actual source of inspiration of these permanent things is thought, this does not prevent their being things. The thought process no more produces anything tangible than the sheer ability to use tools produces objects. It is the reification that occurs in writing something down, painting an image, composing a piece of music, etc. which actually *makes* the thought a reality; and in order to produce these thought-things, which we usually call artworks, the same workmanship is required that through the primordial instrument of human hands builds the other less durable and more useful things of the human artifice.

The man-made world of things becomes a home for mortal men, whose stability will endure and outlast the ever-changing movement of their lives and deeds, only insofar as it transcends both the sheer functionalism of consumer goods and the sheer utility of use-objects. Life in its non-biological sense, that is, the span of time each man is given between birth and death, manifests itself in action and speech, to which now we will turn our attention. With world and deed we insert ourselves into the human world, and this insertion is like a second birth, in which we confirm and take upon ourselves the naked fact of our original physical appearance. Since through birth we came into being, we share with all other entities the quality of *otherness*, an important aspect of plurality that makes it possible for us to define only by distinction: we are unable to say what anything *is* without distinguishing it from something else. In addition to this we share with all living organisms distinguishing marks that make us individual entities. However, only man can *express* otherness and individuality, only he can distinguish and communicate *himself*, and not merely some affect – thirst or hunger, affection or hostility, or fear. In man, otherness and distinctness become uniqueness, for what he inserts with word and deed into the company of his kind is unique. This insertion is not forced upon us through necessity like labor and it is not prompted by wants and desires like work. It has no such conditions; its impulse springs from the beginning that came into the world when we were born and to which we respond by beginning something new of our own initiative. To act, in its most general sense, means to initiate, to begin, as the Greek word *archein* indicates, or to set something into motion, which is the original meaning of the Latin *agere*.

All human activities are conditioned by the fact of human plurality, that not one man, but men in the plural inhabit the earth and in one way or another live together. But only action and speech relate specifically to this fact, to live always means to live among men, among those who are my equals. Hence, when I insert myself into the world, it is a world where others are already present. Action and speech are so closely related because the primordial and specifically human act must always also answer the question asked of every newcomer: 'Who are you?' The disclosure of 'who somebody is' is implicit in the fact that speechless action somehow does not exist, or if it exists it is irrelevant; without speech, action loses the actor, and the doer of deeds is possible only to the extent that he is at the same time the speaker of the words, who identifies himself as the actor and announces what he is doing, what he has done, or what he intends to do. It is exactly as Dante once said – and more succinctly than I could (*De Monarchia*, I, 13): 'For in every action what is primarily intended by the doer . . . is the disclosure of his own image. Hence it comes about that every doer, in so far as he does, takes delight in doing; since everything that is desires its own being, and since in action the being of the doer is somehow intensified, delight necessarily follows . . . Thus nothing acts unless by acting it makes patent its latent self.' To be sure, the disclosure of 'who' always remains hidden from the person himself – like the *daimon* in Greek religion who accompanies man throughout his life, always peering over his shoulder from behind and thus visible only to those he encounters. Still, though unknown to the person, action is intensely personal. Action without a name, a 'who' attached to it, is meaningless whereas an artwork retains its relevance whether or not we know the master's name. Let me remind you of the monuments to the Unknown Soldier after World War I. They bear testimony to the need for finding a 'who', an identifiable somebody whom four years of mass slaughter should have revealed. The unwillingness to resign oneself to the brutal fact that the agent of the war was actually *nobody* inspired the erection of monuments to the unknown ones – that is to all those whom the war had failed to make known, robbing them thereby, not of their achievement, but of their human dignity.

Wherever men live together, there exists a web of human relationships which is, as it were, woven by the deeds and words of innumerable persons, by the living as well as by the dead. Every deed and every new beginning falls into an already existing web, where it nevertheless somehow starts a new process that will affect many others even beyond those with whom the agent comes into direct contact. It is because of this already existing web of human relationships with its conflicting wills and intentions, that action almost never achieves its purpose. And it is also because of this medium and the attendant quality of unpredictability that action always produces stories, with or without intention, as naturally as fabrication produces tangible things. These stories may then be recorded in documents and monuments, they may be told in poetry and historiography, and worked into all kinds of material. They themselves, however, are of an entirely different nature from these reifications. They tell us more about their subjects, the 'hero' in each story, than any product the human hands ever tell us about the master who produced it, and yet they are not products properly speaking. Although everybody starts his own story, at least his own life story, nobody is the author or producer of it. And yet, it is precisely in these stories that the actual meaning of a human life finally reveals itself. That every individual life between birth and death can eventually be told as a story with beginning and end is the pre-political and pre-historical condition of history, the great story without beginning and end. But the reason why each human life tells its story and why history ultimately becomes the storybook of mankind, with many actors and speakers and yet without any recognizable author, is that both are the outcome of action. The real story in which we are engaged as long as we live has no visible or invisible maker because it is not *made*.

The absence of a maker in this realm accounts for the extraordinary frailty and unreliability of strictly human affairs. Since we always act into a web of relationships, the consequences of each deed are boundless, every action touches off not only a reaction but a chain reaction, every process is the cause of unpredictable new processes. This boundlessness is inescapable; it could not be cured by restricting one's acting to a limited graspable framework or circumstances or by feeding all pertinent material into giant computers. The smallest act in the most limited circumstances bears the seed of the same boundlessness and unpredictability; one deed, one gesture, one word may suffice to change every constellation. In acting, in contradistinction to working, it is indeed true that we can really never know what we are doing.

There stands however in stark contrast to this frailty and unreliability of human affairs another character of human action which seems to make it even more dangerous than we would otherwise assume. And this is the simple fact that, though we don't know what we are doing when we are acting, we have no possibility ever to undo what we have done. The processes of action are not only unpredictable, they are also irreversible, which is to say that in action there is no author or maker who can undo or destroy what he has done if he does not like it or when the consequences prove disastrous. This peculiar resiliency of action, apparently in opposition to the frailty of its results, would be altogether unbearable if this capability had not some remedy within its own range.

The possible redemption from the predicament of irreversibility is the faculty of forgiving, and the remedy for unpredictability is contained in the faculty to make and keep promises. The two remedies belong together: forgiving relates to the past and serves to undo its deeds, while binding oneself through promises serves to establish in the ocean of future uncertainty islands of security without which continuity, let alone durability, of any kind, would ever be possible in the relationships between men. Without being forgiven, released from the consequences of what we have done, our capacity to act would, as it were, be confined to one single deed from which we could never recover; we would remain the victims of its consequences forever, not unlike the sorcerer's apprentice who lacked the magic formula to break the spell. Without being bound to the fulfillment of promises, we would never be able to achieve the identity and continuity which together produce the 'person' about whom a story can be told; each of us would be condemned to wander helplessly and without any direction in the darkness of his own lonely heart, caught in its ever-changing moods, contradictions, and equivocalities. But this personal identity, achieved through binding oneself in promises, must be distinguished from the 'objective', i.e., object-related, identity that arises out of being confronted with the sameness of chairs and houses, which I mentioned in the earlier discussion of work. In this respect, forgiving and making promises are like control mechanisms built into the very faculty to start new and endless processes.

Without action, without the capacity to start something new and thus articulate the new beginning that comes into the world with the birth of each human being, the life of man, spent between birth and death, would inevitably be doomed beyond salvation. The life span itself would be running towards death, inevitably carrying everything human to ruin and destruction. Action, with all its uncertainties, is like an ever-present reminder that men, though they must die, are not born in order to die but in order to begin something new. *Initium ut esset homo creatus est* – 'that there be a beginning man was created,' said Augustine. With the creation of man, the principle of beginning came into the world – which, of course is only another way of saying that with the creation of man, the principle of freedom appeared on earth.

1964

Freedom And Politics, A Lecture

I

To speak of the relation between freedom and politics in a lecture is permissible only because a book would be just about as inadequate. For freedom, which only very seldom – in times of crisis or revolution – becomes the direct aim of political action, is actually the reason why such a thing as politics exists in the communal life of man. By freedom, I do not mean that endowment of human nature that the philosophers define one way or another, and like to locate one way or another within human capabilities. Still less do I mean that so-called inner freedom, into which men may escape from external coercion; this is historically a late and objectively a secondary phenomenon. It was originally the result of an estrangement from the world, in which certain worldly experiences and claims were transformed into experiences within one's own self, despite the fact that they came from the outer world and we would have known nothing of them had we not first encountered them as worldly, tangible realities. We first become aware of freedom and its opposite in our intercourse with others, not in intercourse with ourselves. People can only be free in relation to one another, and so only in the realm of politics and action can they experience freedom positively, which is more than *not being forced*.

One cannot speak about politics without also speaking about freedom; and one cannot speak about freedom without also speaking about politics. Where men live together but do not form a body politic – as, for example, in primitive tribal societies or in the privacy of the household – the factor ruling their activities is not freedom but the necessities of life and concern for its preservation. Moreover, wherever the man-made world does not become the scene for political action – as in despotically ruled communities that banish their subjects to the narrowness of the home and private concerns – freedom has no worldly reality. Without a politically guaranteed public realm, freedom lacks the worldly space to make its appearance. To be sure, it may always dwell in men's hearts as a yearning, no matter what their living conditions may be; but it is still not a demonstrable fact in the world. As demonstrably real, freedom and politics coincide and are related to each other as two sides of the same medal.

Yet there is good reason why, today, we cannot take this coincidence of politics and freedom for granted. Since we have become acquainted with forms of total domination, popular opinion holds that nothing is better suited to complete and total abolition of freedom than the total politicization of life. Seen from the perspective of this most recent experience, which naturally we must always keep in mind for considerations of this sort, we must not only doubt the coincidence of politics and freedom, but also their very compatibility. We are inclined to believe that freedom begins where politics ends, because we have seen that freedom disappeared where politics became endless and limitless. The less politics, so it seems, the more freedom, or: the smaller the space occupied by the political, the larger the domain left to freedom. Indeed, it is quite natural for us to measure the extent of freedom in any given community by the free scope it grants to apparently non-political activities, free economic enterprise, for example, or freedom of academic teaching, of religion, or of cultural and intellectual activities. We believe that politics is compatible with freedom only insofar as it guarantees a possible freedom *from* politics.

This definition of political liberty as a potential freedom from politics that is urged upon us by our most recent experiences has also played as large a role in the history of political theory. We find it above all with the political thinkers of the seventeenth and eighteenth centuries, who more often than not simply identified political freedom with security. The purpose of politics was to guarantee security, which, in turn, made freedom possible as something non-political, as a catch-all for activities occurring outside the political realm. Even Montesquieu, though he had a different and much higher opinion of the essence of politics than Hobbes or Spinoza, could still occasionally equate political freedom with security. The rise of the political sciences and political economy in the nineteenth and twentieth centuries even widened the breach between freedom and politics. Government, which since the beginning of the modern age had been identified with the entire domain of the political, was now considered to be the appointed protector not so much of freedom as of the life process and the life interests of society and its individuals. Here, too, security remains the decisive criterion, but what this security is supposed to achieve is not freedom but the uninterrupted process of life. That process, because it is ruled by necessity, has nothing to do with freedom in its real sense. Here freedom has become a marginal phenomenon, in that it forms the boundary that politics is not permitted to over-step, unless life itself and its immediate interests and necessities are at stake.

Thus not only we, who have often become most distrustful of politics when freedom is closest to our hearts, but the entire modern age have separated freedom from politics. Still, I think you all believed you were hearing nothing more than an old truism when I said at the beginning of these remarks that the 'reason why' of politics is freedom. The basis for this is historical as well as factual. To the historical belongs what is really an astounding fact, that in all European languages we use a word for politics in which its origin, the Greek *polis*, can still be heard. Not only etymologically, and not only for scholars, this word is drenched with associations stemming from the community where politics in its specific sense was first discovered. It is thanks to this linguistic usage and its associations that, however far we may have distanced ourselves from the polis, in one crucial respect we have never given up its manner of thinking about politics, namely, in the unanimous opinion of all statesmen and all theoreticians of the Western world, that tyranny is the worst of all forms of state. For this opinion is not self-evident, and there is nothing essential about it, apart from the fact that among classical forms of government tyranny is the only one that in principle cannot be reconciled with freedom. If we really believed, as the theories of the modern age attempt to convince us, that in politics security and life interests are all that is at stake, we would have no reason to reject tyranny; for it can certainly deliver security, and it has often proved itself superior to all other forms of state in protecting mere life. Thus at least in this negative sense, the original coincidence of freedom and politics, which was self-evident to classical antiquity, but not since then, has survived.

Our most recent experiences with totalitarian dictatorships seem suitable to me for confirming anew these oldest experiences with the political. For they have, clearly shown us, if one is serious about the abolition of political freedom, that it is not sufficient to prohibit what we generally understand by political rights; that it is not enough to forbid citizens from being politically active, expressing opinions in public, or forming parties or other associations for the purpose of action. One must also destroy freedom of thought, as far as this is possible, and it is possible to a large extent; one must destroy the freedom of the will; and even the harmless-seeming freedom of artistic production. One must take possession of even those areas we are accustomed to regard as outside the realm of politics, precisely because they, too, contain a political element. Or to put it another way: if one wants to prevent humans from acting in freedom, they must be prevented from thinking, willing and producing, because all these activities imply action, and thereby freedom in every sense, including the political. Therefore, I also believe we entirely misunderstand totalitarianism if we think of it as the total politicization of life through which freedom is destroyed. The exact opposite is the case; we are dealing with the abandonment of politics, as in all dictatorships and despotic regimes, though only in totalitarianism do the phenomena of this abandonment appear in such a radical form as to destroy the element of political freedom in all activities, rather than resting content with stamping out action, the political faculty *par excellence*.

Even this view of things, alienating as it perhaps may be, is still entirely in accordance with traditional political thought. Montesquieu, for example, believes the sign of a free nation is people making any use at all of their reason (*raisonner*), and that, no matter whether they do this well or badly, the fact that they are thinking is enough to bring about freedom. Therefore it is characteristic of despotic regimes that the principle of domination is put in jeopardy as soon as people begin to reason – even if they then try to mount a theoretical justification of tyranny. This has nothing to do with truth, or any other by-product of thinking; it is the sheer activity of reasoning itself from which freedom arises. Reasoning creates a space between men in which freedom is real. Now, again according to Montesquieu, the curious thing about this freedom that arises from the activity of reasoning is that it provides protection against the results of Reason (*raisonnement*), for where freedom, or rather the space for freedom between people engendered by reasoning, is destroyed, as is the case in all tyrannical forms of state, the results of reasoning can only be pernicious. Which is to say, where freedom has stopped being a worldly reality, freedom as an individual's subjective capacity can only lead to ruin, as modern dictators understand only too well. They cannot permit freedom of thought – as the events following Stalin's death have shown – even if they want to.

So there is a wealth of associations that come into play when we hear about freedom and politics; these include the oldest historical memories that have deposited themselves in our language, as well as the tradition of political thought, and the experiences of the present that we consciously keep in mind. Taken all together, they make possible an understanding that goes far beyond contemporary political theory and its conceptual framework. They presuppose a different consciousness of freedom and a different concept of politics to those we are accustomed to, and over which we must now tarry for a while.

II

The relationship between politics and freedom is not a matter of free will or freedom of choice, the *liberum arbitrium* that decides between two given things, one good and one evil as, for example, Richard III's 'I am determined to prove a villain.' Rather it is, to remain with Shakespeare, the freedom of Brutus: 'That this shall be or we fall for it,' that is, the freedom to call something into being which did not exist before, which was not given, not even as object of cognition or imagination, and which therefore could not be known. What guides this action is not a future aim that is conceived by the imagination and can then be seized by the will. The action is guided by something altogether different, which Montesquieu, in his analysis of forms of government, calls a principle. The principle inspires the action, but it cannot prescribe a particular result, as if it were a matter of carrying out a program; it does not manifest itself in any kind of results, but only in the performance of the act itself. In this performance, willing and acting are concurrent, they are one and the same; willing does not prepare for action, it is already the deed. And the action does not execute an act of will; what is manifest is not a subjective will and its end-in-view, but a guiding principle that remains manifest as long as the action lasts. Such principles are honor, glory, or distinguishing oneself above everyone else – the Greek *αἰὲν ἀριστεύειν* – but also fear, distrust, or hatred. Freedom, by contrast, is not a predicate of these principles, and it is located neither in the will nor elsewhere in human nature; rather, it coincides with the action: men are free as long as they act, neither before nor after; for to *be* free and so act are the same.

To illustrate to you what I mean by freedom as inherent in action, I would like to remind you that Machiavelli rediscovered this aspect of freedom, which was specific to antiquity, before Montesquieu, and formulated it conceptually. His *virtù*, which answers to the *fortuna* of the world, is not the Roman *virtus*, nor what we understand by virtue. It is perhaps best translated as 'virtuosity', that is, an excellence we attribute to the performing arts, where the accomplishment lies in the performance itself, and not to the creative or 'making' arts, where an end product outlasts the activity and becomes independent of it. This virtuosity of Machiavelli's *virtù* has much more in common with the Greek ἀρετή, although Machiavelli barely knew the Greeks. He hardly knew they always used metaphors such as flute playing, dancing, healing, and seafaring to describe what was specific to political action, that is, those arts in which virtuosity of performance is the decisive quality.

Because action demands virtuosity and virtuosity is peculiar to the performing arts, politics in general has often been defined as an art. This is completely false if one falls into the common error of taking the word art to refer to the creative, productive arts, and regards the state or government as a work of art – even as the greatest artwork human hands have ever produced. In the sense of the productive arts bringing forth something tangible that both lasts beyond and completely breaks free from the activity that called it into being, politics is the exact opposite of an art – which incidentally does not mean it is a science. The state is not an artwork for the very reason that its existence never becomes independent of the human actions that brought it into being.

Independent existence marks the work of art as a product of making; dependence upon further action to keep it in existence marks the state as a product of action. And the similarity between action and the performing arts goes still further. Just as the virtuosity of music making or dancing or theater is dependent upon an audience to experience the performance, action also requires the presence of others in a politically organized space. Such a space is not to be taken for granted wherever men live together in a community. The Greek polis once was precisely that 'form of government' necessary for action.

If we understand the political in the sense of the Greek polis – to which were admitted only people who were neither slaves, subject to coercion by others, not laborers, driven by the necessity of the biological process of life – it represents the space where this freedom as action, properly understood as virtuosity, can appear. In the public, political realm, freedom is a worldly reality, there it can become real in words, deeds, and events that then can be remembered and incorporated into human history. Whatever occurs in this space of appearances is political by definition, even if it has nothing directly to do with action. What remains outside it, such as the great feats of barbarian empires, may be impressive and noteworthy but, strictly speaking, not political. Without such a space established for it, freedom cannot be realized. There is no actual freedom without politics; It simply could not exist. On the other hand, a community that is not a space for the appearance of the endless variations of the virtuosity in which being free manifests itself, is not political.

These conceptions of freedom and politics and their relation to one another seem so strange to us because we usually understand freedom either as freedom of thought or of the will, and because we ascribe to politics the task of providing the necessities of life, which ensure the security of human existence and the safeguarding of its interests. But in this, too, there is a basic conviction that rings very familiar and self-evident, and which is only forgotten when we start to theorize on these matters. It is the age-old conviction that courage is the cardinal virtue in political behavior. Courage is a big word, and I do not mean the foolhardy type of courage that welcomes danger and gladly risks life for the sake of the intense thrill which danger and the possibility of death evoke. Recklessness is no less concerned with life than is cowardice. Courage, which we still believe to be indispensable for political action, does not gratify our individual sense of vitality but is demanded of us by the very nature of the public realm. For in contrast to our private domain where, in the protection of family and the privacy of our own four walls, everything serves and must serve the security of the life process, there stands the public realm, which is common to all, if only because it existed before us and is meant to outlast us, and simply cannot afford to give primary concern to individual lives and the elementary interests associated with them. It requires courage in the political sense to step out into this public realm – not because of particular dangers that may lie in wait for us there, but because we have arrived in a realm where care for life has lost its validity. Courage liberates men from their care for life for the sake of the freedom of the world. Courage is required because in the politics the primary care is never for life itself, but always for the world, which will outlast all of us, in one form or another.

Those for whom the word 'politics' conjures up the idea of freedom therefore cannot feel that the political is only the sum total of private interests and the balancing out of their conflicts; nor that the state's attitude towards the entire population of its territory is the same as that of paterfamilias toward the members of his family. In both instances, politics is incompatible with freedom. Freedom can be the meaning of politics only if the political designates a realm that is public and therefore not only distinguished from, but also opposed to the private realm and its interests.

In theory, the conception of the public, statelike realm of political entity, for example a nation, as one vast family, a gigantic household, is very old; however, it has only gained practical significance since modern society pushed its way between the politico-public and the purely private spheres, and blurred the boundaries between them. It is in the social no-man's-land that all of us now live, and modern political theories, whether liberal, conservative, or socialist, are all in essence about society, the peculiar structures of which (though I cannot go into these now) essentially privatize matters of public interest, and publicize matters of private concern. Furthest advanced along this path are, of course, the totalitarian dictatorships, which, as we all know, boast that they have abolished the difference between public and private life and the conflict between public and private interests, in favor of an instrumentalism of force and terror, which replaces the interests of the social collective as a whole. But in the Western democracies, too, the boundaries between public and private life have become blurred, though in a different way; here the party politicians boast that they represent the private interests of their electorate in the same way a good lawyer represents his clients; as a result, the public realm, the world surrounding us, is again riddled with individual, private interests. The sciences of this society, the social sciences, are familiar to you all, and, from behaviorism to proletarian Marxism, they all aim at one and the same thing, namely, to prevent the acting man in his freedom from interfering in the movement and course of events. In terms of the problem we are considering, it is immaterial whether the socialization of men happens in the sense of behaviorism, which reduces all actions to the behavior of atomized individuals, or in the much more radical sense of the modern ideologies that reduce all political events and actions to a society's historical process and its own laws. The difference between this widely held ideological thinking and total domination is that the latter has discovered the means by which it can absorb men into the social stream of history in such a way that they no longer have any desire to interfere with its automatic flow, but on the contrary, add their own momentum to accelerate it further. The means by which this is achieved are the compulsion imposed by a regime of terror from without, and the compulsion of an ideological way of thinking imposed from within. There is no doubt that this totalitarian development is a crucial step toward both the abandonment of politics by men, and the abolishment of freedom; though theoretically speaking, freedom starts to disappear wherever the concepts of society and history have ousted the concept of politics.

III

We have seen that the assertion: 'The meaning of politics is freedom' presupposes that the political is concerned with the world as such and not with life, and that freedom begins where concern for life ceases to compel men to behave in a specific manner. And we have seen that this notion of an interdependence of freedom and politics stands in contradiction to the social theories of the modern age. This state of affairs seems like an invitation to try and go back beyond the modern age and its theories and to put our faith in older traditions. But the real difficulty in reaching an understanding of what freedom is arises from the fact that a simple return to tradition does not help us. For my assertion that freedom is, in essence, a political phenomenon, that it is not experienced primarily in will and thought, but in action, and that therefore it requires a sphere appropriate to such action, a political sphere, is in direct contradiction to some very ancient and highly respected concepts. Neither the philosophical concept of freedom as it first arose in late antiquity, where freedom became a phenomenon of thought, nor the Christian and modern notion of free will, are political in nature; indeed, both contain a strongly antipolitical element, which is by no means a foible of philosophers or *homines religiosi*, but is based upon human experience of the highest authenticity in politics itself. We must content ourselves here with recalling that, in answer to our query regarding the relation between politics and freedom, tradition is all but unanimous in saying that freedom begins when a man withdraws from communal life, from the political sphere, and that he experiences freedom not in association with others but in intercourse with himself – whether in the form of an inner dialogue which, since the time of Socrates, we have called thinking, or as a conflict within himself, in the struggle between the I-will and I-can, as Christianity after Paul and Augustine thought to discern the inadequacy and questionable value of human freedom.

As regards the problem of freedom, it is natural for us to examine it and seek our answers within the framework of Christian tradition. That we must do so is indicated by the simple fact that for the most part, and quite automatically, we think of freedom as free will, that is, as the predicate of a factually virtually unknown to classical antiquity. For will, as Christianity discovered it, had so little in common with the simple desire to possess some eagerly longed-for object that it could even come into conflict with such impulse. If freedom were actually nothing but a phenomenon of the will, we would have to conclude that it was unknown to the ancients. Such a conclusion, of course, is absurd, but if someone wished to assert it he could argue that the idea of freedom played no role in the works of the great philosophers prior to Augustine. The reason for this striking fact is that in the ancient world freedom was regarded exclusively and radically as a political concept, indeed as the quintessence of the city-state and citizenship, the βίοςπολιτιχός, the political way of life. But our own philosophical tradition, beginning with Parmenides and Plato, was founded in opposition to the polis and the political realm. That ancient philosophy should not have taken up the subject of freedom, which is the most political of all ancient concepts, is entirely understandable. It could not have been otherwise before Christianity discovered in free will a non-political freedom, which could be experienced in intercourse with oneself, and was therefore not dependent upon intercourse with the many.

In view of the extraordinary potential power inherent in the will, we tend to forget that it originally did not manifest itself as I-will-and-I-can, but on the contrary, as a conflict between the two; and it was this conflict that was unknown to antiquity. The conception of the I-will-and-I-can was of course very familiar to the ancients. I need only remind you how Plato insisted that only those who knew how to rule and obey themselves had the right to rule others, and to be free from any obligation to obey them. The self-control, or alternatively, the conviction that self-control alone justifies the exercise of authority, has remained the hallmark of the aristocratic outlook to this very day. And in fact it is a typically political virtue, a phenomenon of virtuosity where the I-will and the I-can must be so well attuned that they practically coincide. But when we separate the I-will and I-can, we are speaking in contradictory terms from the viewpoint of the Christian conception of free will. Had ancient philosophy known of this separation, it would certainly have understood freedom as an inherent quality of the I-can, rather than the I-will. Wherever the I-can foundered, be it as the result of extraneous circumstance or of individual circumstance, there would have been no talk of freedom.

I chose the example of self-control because to us this is clearly a phenomenon which can be explained only in terms of the will. The Greeks, as you know, gave much thought to the question of moderation and the necessity of steering and taming the steeds of the soul; yet among all those phenomena, which to us are manifestation of the will's strength, the Greeks never discovered the will as a distinct faculty, separate from other human faculties, something, indeed, of a specific and exceptional quality in man. It is a historical fact, which is well worth pondering, that men became explicitly aware of the existence of the will when they experienced its impotence and not its power, and began to say with St Paul: 'For to will is present with me; but how to perform that which is good I find not.' For us, the essential point is that this was not a case of the impotence of man's will in the world. The will was not defeated by some overwhelming force of nature or circumstance, or the conflict of one against many; it was solely the impotence of the will in the individual man. All willing springs from the original conflict in man between his will and the ability to do what he wills; this means, literally, that the I-will strikes back at the self, spurs it on, incites it to action or is ruined by it. This bondage of the will to the self persists, even if a man sets out to conquer the whole world; moreover, and as a matter of principle, it divides the I-will from the I-think – which also implies a self-reflective quality, though in this instance the self is not also the object of the dialogue. Perhaps it is because the will's impotence first made us aware of its existence that it has now become so unusually power-hungry that the will and the will-to-power have become practically synonymous to our ears. Tyranny at any rate, the only form of government that arises from the singularity of the I-will and its absolute egoism, is incomparably more greedy and cruel than the utopian governments of reason, with which the philosophers wished to coerce men and which they conceived on the model of the I-think.

I have said that the philosophers first began to show an interest in freedom when freedom was no longer experienced in acting and in associating with others but in willing as intercourse with one's self. The fact the freedom was thus transformed from a primarily political fact into a philosophical problem of the first order naturally did not prevent this new philosophical problematic from subsequently being applied to the political realm. But now that the emphasis had shifted so decisively from action to willpower, the ideal of freedom ceased to be the virtuosity of acting in concert with others and became sovereignty, the independence from others and the ability, if necessary, to prevail against them. Politically, perhaps no other element of the traditional philosophical concept of freedom has proved as pernicious as this equation of freedom with sovereignty that is inherent in it. For this leads either to a denial of freedom – when it is realized that whatever men may be, they are not sovereign – or to the insight, which may seem to contradict this denial but does not, that the freedom of one man or a group can only be purchased at the price of the freedom of others. What is so extraordinarily difficult to understand within this problematic relation is a simple fact, namely, that freedom is only given to men under the condition of nonsovereignty. Moreover, it is as unrealistic to deny freedom because of human nonsovereignty as it is dangerous to believe that one alone – as an individual or an organized group – can be free only if that one is sovereign. Even the sovereignty of a political body is always an illusion which, moreover, can be maintained only by means of violence.

Admittedly, in order properly to understand how unreal and pernicious this identification of freedom and sovereignty is, one must liberate oneself from an old prejudice that goes as far back as the Roman *stoa*. This prejudice is the view that nonsovereignty is the same as dependence, which would mean that the nonsovereignty of human existence would be simply the fact that humans need each other to remain alive. The dependence of human beings upon one another in all questions of mere life is evident; it is sealed in the fact of birth, insofar as humans, as the Greeks say, are born ἐξ ἀλλήλων, out of each other. But *this* dependent quality of human life applies only to the individual; it need not apply to a group that has absolute power over others, or else is powerful and moderate enough to isolate itself from all others. But far more decisive than this dependence of an individual is that man in the singular cannot be imagined, that men's existence as a whole depends upon there always being others of their kind. Were there only *one* man, as we say there is only *one* God, then the concept of humanity as we know it would not exist; if there was only *one* nation on earth, or only *one* people, then of course no man would know what a nation or a people is. Being among one's own kind ends only with death, as the Latin implies so well, equating *inter homines esse* (to be among men) with 'life' and *desinere inter homines esse* (to cease to be among men) with 'death'. Only in death, or in the face of death, can human existence become entirely singular.

Like the sovereignty of the individual, the sovereignty of a group or a political body is, as has been noted, also an illusion, for it can come about only if a great many people behave as if they were *one*, and indeed the *only* one. Such behavior is certainly possible, as we know only too well from the many phenomena of mass society, which also demonstrate that there is no freedom in such society. Where everyone does the same, nobody acts in freedom, even when nobody is directly coerced or compelled. In human relationships, then, which are governed by the fact that there are only *men*, and not *man*, only many peoples, and not a single people, freedom and sovereignty are so little identical that they cannot even exist simultaneously. Where men, whether as individuals or in organized groups, wish to be sovereign, they must abolish freedom. But if they wish to be free, it is precisely sovereignty they must renounce.

To illustrate how difficult it is within the conceptual structure of our philosophical tradition to formulate a concept of freedom that conforms with political experience, I want to look at two modern thinkers who, in terms of both political philosophy and theory, are perhaps the greatest and most profound – namely, Montesquieu and Kant.

Montesquieu is so aware of the inadequacies of the philosophical tradition in these matters that he expressly distinguishes between philosophical and political freedom. The difference is that philosophy demands no more of freedom than the exercise of the will (*l'exercice de la volonté*), independent of circumstances in the world and of attainment of the goals the will sets for itself. Political freedom, by contrast, is the security (*la liberté politique consiste dans la sûreté*) that does not exist always and everywhere, but only in political communities governed by laws. Without security there is no political freedom, for freedom means 'being able to do what one ought to will' (*la liberté ne peut consister qu'à pouvoir faire ce que l'on doit vouloir*). As obvious as these sentences make Montesquieu's propensity to juxtapose the philosophical freedom of a willing self with *being* free politically, a worldly, tangible reality, his dependency on the philosophical tradition of free will is no less evident. For Montesquieu's definitions sound as if political freedom is nothing but an extension of philosophical freedom, namely, the freedom that is indispensable for the realization of the freedom of an I-will. If we want to understand Montesquieu's real intentions, however, we must take the trouble to read his sentences so that the emphasis does not fall on the I-*can* – the notion that one must be able to do what one wants or should want – but on the deed. It should be added that actions and deeds are viewed here as considerably more significant than the quasi-automatic fulfillment of the will. Freedom itself is enacted in actions, and the security that guarantees the ability to perform them is provided by others. This freedom does not reside in an I-will, which the I-can may either comply with or contradict without bringing man's philosophical freedom into question; political freedom begins only in action, so that not-being-able-to-act and not-being-free amount to one and the same thing, even if philosophy's free will continues to exist intact. In other words, political freedom is not 'inner freedom'; it cannot hide inside a person. It is dependent on a free people to grant it the space in which actions can appear, be seen, and be effective. The power of the self-assertion of the will to compel others has nothing whatever to do with this political freedom.

In Kant, the only one among the great philosophers for whom the question 'What should I do?' held the same dignity as the specifically philosophical questions: 'What can I know? What may I hope?' The strength of the antipolitical tradition in philosophy does not show itself in insufficient formulations as it does in Montesquieu, but in the remarkable fact that in Kant there are two very different political philosophies: the one that is generally accepted as such in the *Critique of Practical Reason*, and the other in the *Critique of Judgment*. The literature on Kant rarely mentions that the first part of the *Critique of Judgment* is actually a philosophy of politics. I believe one can, however, demonstrate that in all his political writings the theme of judgment carried more weight for Kant than did that of practical reason. Freedom appears in the *Critique of Judgment* as a predicate of the imagination, not of the will, and the imagination is most intimately related to that 'enlarged mentality', which is the political way of thinking *par excellence*, because through it we have the possibility 'to think in the position of everyone else'. Only in this context does it become philosophically clear why Kant was able to say emphatically: 'The external force that wrenches away people's public freedom to communicate their thoughts also takes from them their freedom to think.' Here, being unfree retaliates against the 'inner' ability to be free and destroys it. Even freedom of thought, as Kant puts it, the inner 'conversation with oneself' depends, if it is to issue in thoughts, on the presence of others and thus on the opportunity to 'advance our thoughts in public to see whether they agree with the understanding of others'.

But this concept of freedom as entirely independent of free will has played hardly any role in the reception of Kant's philosophy. And even in Kant's philosophy itself it is overshadowed by that of 'practical reason' which ascribes to the will, for good or evil, all power in human affairs, while action itself, as you will remember, no longer falls within the sphere of human power and freedom, but is subordinate to necessity and subject to the law of causality. To be free only as long as one can will, means only as long as the I-will is not opposed by an inner I-can*not*, which in turn means that one becomes unfree as soon as one begins to act. Kant had hardly any doubt about these two fundamental propositions in the narrower sense of his practical-political philosophy.

IV

We find it difficult to understand that there may exist a freedom that is not an attribute of the will but of doing and acting. For us, the whole problem of freedom is overshadowed by Christianity and an originally antipolitical philosophic tradition. In order now to define more precisely this freedom that is experienced in the process of acting and nothing else, let us go back once more to antiquity – not for the sake of erudition, or even the continuity of our tradition, but merely in order to grasp the experiences that, although we are all somehow familiar with them, have never again been articulated with the same classical clarity.

The first thing that must strike us is that both Greek and Latin have two words for the verb 'to act', which denote two very different processes. The two Greek words are ἄρχειν (to begin, to lead, and to rule) and πράττειν (to carry something through). The corresponding Latin verbs are *agere*: to set something in motion, and *gerere* which is hard to translate and somehow means the enduring and supporting continuation of past acts that result in the *res gestae*, the deeds and events we call historical. In both instances, the first stage of action is a beginning, by which something new comes into the world. The fact that freedom was originally experienced in this ability to make a new beginning, in what since Kant we have come to call spontaneity, can be seen in the range of meanings of the Greek word, where, as I mentioned, beginning is conjoined with leading and finally ruling, the outstanding qualities of the free man. This manifold meaning of ἄρχειν indicates that beginning something new could only fall to someone who was already a ruler, and in Greece this meant a man who presided over a household of slaves, liberating him from the necessities of life, and who was thus free to live in the polis among his peers; but beginning itself coincides with leading others, for only with the help of others could the beginner carry through (πράττειν) whatever he had started to do.

In Latin, to be free and to begin are also interconnected, though in a different way. Roman freedom was a legacy bequeathed by the founders of Rome to the Roman people; their freedom was tied to the beginning their forefathers established by founding the city, and with it Roman history. The descendants had to conduct their forefathers' affairs, bear their consequences (*gerere*), and by the same token augment Rome's foundations (*res gestae*). Roman historiography therefore, though essentially as political as Greek historiography, never was content with commending to the memory of the citizens certain great events and stories, as Thucydides and Herodotus had done; Roman historians were always bound to the beginning of Roman history, because this beginning contained the authentic element that made their history political. Whatever the Romans had to relate, they started *ab urbe condita*, with the foundation of the city, the ultimate guarantee of Roman freedom.

To go one step further, we can say that the

intrinsic meaning of the political in antiquity is intimately linked with this ability to begin. There is a good reason why the ancients found it literally impossible to think of the political without the city. Only the founding of a city could provide a beginning and set something in motion, could give rise to the ἄρχειν and *agere*. The city gave the beginning a reliable chance, because the help of others, which is indispensable for carrying something through, the πράττειν and *gerere*, is always on hand in a regulated community of citizens. Thus the citizens of a polis are in a position to do more than people who have become masters of the necessities of life, and can act from time to time: citizens can always be free. It is in the nature of the city-state's development that over time, performance and continuation take on a greater significance for political life than initiation itself, and the consequence of this is that in both Greek and Latin there eventually came to be only *one* verb for acting, namely πράττειν and *gerere*, while ἄρχειν and *agere*, which did not vanish from the languages, no longer retained their full political meaning. Nevertheless, Aristotle, who in his political philosophy otherwise exclusively uses the word πράττειν to designate the whole sphere of human affairs and activities, says that the polis is made up of ἄρχοντες, and not of πράττοντες. The former carries the meaning of both ruling, namely the ruling of slaves, which makes freedom possible, and the positive freedom of beginning.

I have already mentioned that the ancient concept of freedom, precisely because it was exclusively political, played no role in the philosophy of the Socratic school. Roman writers, it is true, rebelled occasionally against the antipolitical tendencies of the Greek philosophic schools, but they did not go further or decisively change either the themes or the way of thinking in the doctrines handed down to them. And of course they never hit upon a theoretical, philosophical formula for the freedom they had experienced in the political realm. We have even less hope of finding a valid political idea of freedom in Christian philosophy, and maybe least of all in the great Christian thinker Augustine, who made the new 'inner' freedom of the will, which may have been first experienced by Paul, into one of the cornerstones of traditional Western philosophy. Yet in Augustine we find not only the *liberum arbitrium* that has, as the free choice of the will, become definitive for the tradition, but also a notion of freedom conceived in an entirely different manner, which characteristically appears in his only political treatise, *De Civitate Dei*. In *The City of God*, Augustine, as is only natural, speaks more from his background of specifically Roman experiences than in any other of his writings. Freedom is conceived here not as an inner human disposition, but as a term that characterizes human existence in the world, and he founds this freedom in the fact that man is himself a beginning in the world, an *initium*, insofar as he has not existed as long as the world itself, was not created simultaneously with it, but as a new beginning after the world had come into existence. In the birth of each man this initial beginning is reaffirmed, because in each instance something new comes into an already existing world, which will continue to exist after each individual's death. Because he *is* a beginning, says Augustine, man can begin, and thus be free; God created man so that there was such a thing as a beginning in the world: '[*Initium*] *ut esset, creatus est homo, ante quem nullus fuit.*'

The strong antipolitical tendencies of early Christianity are so familiar that the notion of a Christian thinker developing the philosophical implications of the ancient political idea of freedom strikes us as almost paradoxical. Yet this second Augustinian concept of freedom had no effect on the tradition of either Christian or modern philosophy, and we begin to find traces of it again only in Kant's writings. Like Augustine, Kant recognizes two concepts of freedom, conceived completely independently of each other: practical freedom, which he defines as 'the independence of the power of choice from necessitation by impulses of sensibility', which therefore is still a negative freedom; and that 'spontaneity' which, in his philosophy, is especially fundamental to thinking and cognition, and which he defines as the ability to 'begin a series of occurrences entirely from itself'. We can see how closely related this Kantian spontaneity is to Augustine's beginning from the fact that he also calls it 'freedom in the cosmological sense'. If freedom were primarily or exclusively a phenomenon of the will, it would hardly be possible to understand why cognition does not occur apart from the spontaneity of mental concepts, nor why Kant speaks so emphatically about the 'spontaneity of thinking'.

Be that as it may, the fact that we find a philosophical foundation for politically experienced freedom for the first time in the works of a Roman Christian thinker will seem strange only if we orient our idea of Christianity according to the antipolitical bent of ancient Christian thought, in particular the doctrine of the will in the epistles of St Paul. Yet I am convinced that this impression would change considerably if we were to look more intently at Jesus of

Nazareth – the man and his teachings. Here we find a quite extraordinary understanding of freedom and of the power inherent in human freedom; but the human capacity that corresponds to this power and, in the words of the Gospel, is capable of moving mountains, is not will but faith. The work of faith is the 'miracle', a word with many meanings in the New Testament and difficult to understand. We can overlook the difficulties here, however, by referring only to those passages where miracles are not exclusively supernatural events, even though all miracles interrupt some natural series of events or automatic processes, in whose context they constitute the entirely unexpected.

I would like to suggest that, if it is true that action and beginning are essentially the same, it follows that a capacity for performing miracles must likewise be within the range of human faculties. And in order to make this theory a little more palatable, I would like to remind you of the nature of every new beginning: seen from the viewpoint of what has gone before, it breaks into the world unexpected and unforeseen. Fundamentally, every event seems to us like a miracle, and it may well be a prejudice to consider miracles as supernatural only in religious contexts. And in order to explain this in turn, I may perhaps remind you that the whole frame of our real existence – the earth, the organic life on it, the evo-lution of mankind out of animal species – rests on a chain of miracles. From the viewpoint of processes in the universe and their statistically overwhelming probabilities, the formation of the earth is an 'infin-ite improbability', as the natural scientists would say – or a miracle, as we might call it. The same is true for the formation of organic life out of inor-ganic processes, or the evolution of man out of the processes of organic life. In other words, every new beginning becomes a miracle the moment we look at it from the viewpoint of the processes it has inter-rupted. The crucial thing to remember is that this viewpoint is not special or especially sophisticated; it is, on the contrary, most natural and indeed, in ordinary life, almost commonplace.

I chose this example to illustrate that what we call real is always a mesh of earthly-organic-human real-ity, which came into being *qua* reality through the advent of infinite improbabilities. Of course the example has its limitations and cannot be applied to the realm of human affairs ingenuously. For in the political realm historical processes confront us – one event follows another – rather than natural develop-ments with their attendant accidents. The result of this is that the miracle of accident and infinite improbability occurs so frequently in human affairs that it seems strange to speak of miracles at all. However, the reason for this frequency is merely that historical processes are created and constantly interrupted by human initiative. If one considers historical processes only as processes, then every new beginning within them, for better and worse, becomes so infinitely unlikely that all large events appear as miracles. Objectively, seen from the outside, the chances that tomorrow will proceed exactly as today are always overwhelming – not quite so overwhelming, but in human proportions nearly as great as the chances that *no* earth would ever rise out of cosmic events, that *no* life would develop out of inorganic processes, and that *no* man would appear out of the evolution of animal life.

The decisive difference between the 'infinite improbabilities' on which life on earth and the reality of nature rest, and the miraculous events within human affairs, is that in the latter case there is a miracle worker, which is to say that humans appear to have a highly mysterious gift for making miracles happen. This gift is called action. And insofar as action and beginning are the same, there is an element of action in every human activity that is more than a mere reaction. The simple act of production adds a new object to the world, and pure thought always begins a sequence quite by itself.

V

Finally, let us try to find our way back from these philosophical foundations of a politically experienced conception of freedom, which may help orient ourselves briefly in the field of our present political experiences. We can say that the extraordinary danger of totalitarianism for the future of mankind exists less in the fact that it is tyrannical and does not tolerate political freedom, than that it threatens to kill off all forms of spontaneity, that is, the element of action and freedom in all human activities. It is of the essence of this most horrific form of tyranny that it strives to eliminate the possibility of 'miracles' or, to put it more familiarly, to exclude the possibility of events in politics, and thereby deliver us up entirely to the automatic processes that surround us anyhow – in earthly nature as in the universe that surrounds the earth – and by which we ourselves are driven insofar as we are also organic nature. It would be sheer superstition, a negative belief in miracles, to hope for the 'infinitely improbable' in the context of these automatic processes, although even this never can be ruled out completely. But it is not in the least superstitious, it is even a counsel of realism, to look for the unforeseeable, to be prepared for and expect 'miracles' in the political realm, where in fact they are always possible. For human freedom is not merely a matter of metaphysics; it is a matter of fact, as are the automatic processes within and against which it always asserts itself. On the other hand, the processes set in motion by action also tend to become automatic, which means that no single act and no single event can ever redeem or bring salvation to mankind, or a people, once and for all.

It is in the nature of these automatic processes, to which man is subject and, except for the miracle of freedom would be subjected absolutely, that they can only spell ruin for human life. They are ruinous as the biological processes that pervade man's entire being and which, biologically, can only lead from birth to death. Only the world and men in the plural can anticipate salvation through the miracle that is possible in all political affairs – at least as long as freedom, the human gift of interrupting ruin, remains intact. No miracle is required to save life as such since by nature it endures with the species, nor can a miracle ever save man in the singular, who must always die as an individual. These ruinous processes can be interrupted only for the world that is common to us all, which outlasts our life or at least can outlast it, and which is the specific concern of politics. From this it follows that, although the

ability to begin may be a gift of man in his singularity, he can only realize it in relation to the world and
in acting together with his fellow men.

In contrast to thinking and producing, one can
only *act* with the help of others and in the world.
'[To] act in concert,' as Burke puts it, realizes the
ability to begin as *being* free. The difference between
acting on the one hand, and producing and thinking
on the other, is that in producing and thinking only
the beginning is free; the completion, if it is successful, never realizes more than the thought already
grasped at the beginning, or the thing conceived
beforehand by the power of the imagination, both
of which are subject to the processes of production
or thought. By contrast, however little an action
may achieve, the performance of it remains directed
toward the constantly renewed actualization of
freedom, with new beginnings constantly flowing
into what has once been begun. For the result of
action is not an object, which, once it has been conceived, can be produced. The result of action rather
has the character of a story, which continues for as
long as people continue to act, but the end and the
result of which nobody, not even the person who
began the story, can foresee or conceive. In the case
of action, the beginning and performance are therefore not so separate that the person who begins to

act knows everything in advance, while those who help him complete the action need only realize his knowledge, follow his orders, and execute his decisions. In action, beginning and performance merge into each other, and, when applied to politics, this means that the person who takes the initiative and thus starts to lead must always move among those who join in to help him as his peers, and neither as a leader among his servants nor as a master among his apprentices or disciples. This is what Herodotus meant when he said that to be free was neither to rule nor to be ruled, and that therefore men could only be free in *ἰσονομία*, as democracy was originally called, in being among one's equals.

In the state of *being* free, where the gift of freedom, the ability to begin, becomes a tangible worldly reality, the actual space of the political comes into being along with the stories that action generates. This space is always and everywhere that men live together in freedom, without domination or subjugation. But, even if the institutional-organizational framework surrounding it remains intact, this space vanishes immediately if action ceases, and security measures and maintaining the status quo take its place, or if there is a slackening of the initiative to project new beginnings into the processes that action first set in motion. Then the processes that freedom first brought forth also become automatic, and an automatic process produced by men is no less ruinous for the world than automatic natural processes are for the life of the individual. In such cases, historians speak of petrified or declining civilizations, and we know that the processes of decline can go on for centuries. Quantitatively, they occupy by far the largest space in recorded history.

In the history of mankind, the periods of freedom have always been relatively short. By contrast, even in the long epochs of petrification and decline, the sheer ability to begin, the element of freedom inherent in all human activities, can remain intact, and so it is not at all surprising that we tend to define freedom as something that can be realized outside of politics, as freedom *from* politics. Yet this self-understanding is a misunderstanding, which stems from and corresponds to a situation in which everything specifically political has become stagnant or fallen into a presumably inescapable automatism. Under such circumstances, freedom is indeed no longer experienced as a positive activity with its own specific 'virtuosity'. *Being* free then has receded to the gift that only man, among all earthly creatures, seems to have received. Though we find its intimation in nonpolitical activities, that gift can develop fully only where action creates its own worldly space in which freedom can appear.

European man has always known that freedom as a mode of being and a worldly reality can be destroyed, and that only seldom in history has it unfolded its full virtuosity. Now that we are acquainted with totalitarianism we must also suspect that not only *being* free but also the sheer gift of freedom, which was not produced by man but given to him, may be destroyed, too. This knowledge or suspicion weighs more heavily upon us now than ever before, for today, more depends on human freedom than before – on man's ability to tip scales heavily weighted toward disaster, which always happens automatically and therefore always appears irresistible. This time, no less than the continued existence of men on earth may depend upon man's gift of performing 'miracles', that is, bringing about the infinitely improbable and establishing it as a worldly reality.

1960

The Freedom To Be Free

THE CONDITIONS AND
MEANING OF REVOLUTION

My subject today, I'm afraid, is almost embarrassingly topical. Revolutions have become everyday occurrences since, with the liquidation of imperialism, so many peoples have risen 'to assume among the powers of the earth the separate and equal station to which the laws of nature and nature's God entitle them'. Just as the most lasting result of imperialist expansion was the export of the idea of the nation-state to the four corners of the earth, so the end of imperialism under the pressure of nationalism has led to the dissemination of the idea of revolution all over the globe.

All these revolutions, no matter how violently anti-Western their rhetoric may be, stand under the sign of traditional Western revolutions. The current state of affairs was preceded by the series of revolutions after the First World War in Europe itself.

Since then, and more markedly after the Second World War, nothing seems more certain than that a revolutionary change of the form of government, in distinction to an alteration of administration, will follow defeat in a war between the remaining powers – short, that is, of total annihilation. But it is important to note that even before technological developments made wars between the great powers literally a life-and-death struggle, hence self-defeating, politically speaking wars had already become a matter of life and death. This was by no means a matter of course, but signifies that the protagonists of national wars had begun to act as though they were involved in civil wars. And the small wars of the last twenty years – Korea, Algeria, Vietnam – have clearly been civil wars, in which the great powers became involved, either because revolution threatened their rule or had created a dangerous power vacuum. In these instances it was no longer war that precipitated revolution; the initiative shifted from war to revolution, which in some cases, but by no means all, was followed by military intervention. It is as if we were suddenly back in the eighteenth century, when the American Revolution was followed by a war against England, and the French Revolution by a war against the allied royal powers of Europe.

And again, despite the enormously different circumstances – technological and otherwise – military interventions appear relatively helpless in the face of the phenomenon. A large number of revolutions during the last two hundred years went to their doom, but relatively few were dissipated by superiority in the application of the means of violence. Conversely, military interventions, even when they were successful, have often proved remarkably inefficient in restoring stability and filling the power vacuum. Even victory seems unable to substitute stability for chaos, honesty for corruption, authority and trust in government for decay and disintegration. Restoration, the consequence of an interrupted revolution, usually provides not much more than a thin and quite obviously provisional cover under which the processes of disintegration continue unchecked. But there is, on the other hand, a great potential future stability inherent in consciously formed new political bodies, of which the American Republic is the prime example; the principal problem, of course, is the rarity of successful revolutions. Still, in the world's present configuration where, for better or worse, revolutions have become the most significant and frequent events – and this will most likely continue for decades to come – it would not only be wiser but also more relevant if, instead of boasting that we are the mightiest power on earth, we would say that we have enjoyed an extraordinary stability since the founding of our republic, and that this stability was the direct outgrowth of revolution. For, since it can no longer be decided by war, the contestation of the great powers may well be decided, in the long run, by which side better understands what revolutions are and what is at stake in them.

It is, I believe, a secret from nobody, at least not since the Bay of Pigs incident, that the foreign policy of this country has shown itself hardly expert or even knowledgeable in judging revolutionary situations or in understanding the momentum of revolutionary movements. Although the Bay of Pigs is often blamed on faulty information and malfunctioning secret services, the failure actually lies much deeper. The failure was in misunderstanding what it means when a poverty-stricken people in a backward country, in which corruption has reached the point of rottenness, are suddenly released, not from their poverty, but from the obscurity and hence incomprehensibility of their misery; what it means when they hear for the first time their condition being discussed in the open and find themselves invited to participate in that discussion; and what it means when they are brought to their capital, which they have never seen before, and told: these streets and these buildings and these squares, all these are yours, your possessions, and hence your pride. This, or something of the same sort, happened for the first time during the French Revolution. Curiously, it was an old man in East Prussia who never left his hometown of Königsberg, Immanuel Kant, a philosopher and lover of freedom hardly famous for rebellious thoughts, who at once did understand. He said that 'such a phenomenon in human history will never be forgotten,' and indeed, it has not been forgotten but, on the contrary, has played a major role in world history ever since it occurred. And though many revolutions have ended in tyranny, it has also always been remembered that, in the words of Condorcet, 'The word "revolutionary" can be applied only to revolutions whose aim is freedom.'

Revolution, like any other term of our political vocabulary, can be used in a generic sense without taking into account either the word's origin or the temporal moment when the term was first applied to a particular political phenomenon. The assumption of such usage is that no matter when and why the term itself appeared, the phenomenon to which it refers is coeval with human memory. The temptation to use the word generically is particularly strong when we speak of 'wars and revolutions' together, for wars, indeed, are as old as the recorded history of mankind. It may be difficult to use the word war in any other than a generic sense, if only because its first appearance cannot be dated in time or localized in space, but no such excuse exists for the indiscriminate usage of the term revolution. Prior to the two great revolutions at the end of the eighteenth century and the specific sense it then acquired, the word revolution was hardly prominent in the vocabulary of political thought or practice. When the term occurs in the seventeenth century, for example, it clings strictly to its original astronomical meaning, which signified the eternal, irresistible, ever-recurring motion of the heavenly bodies; its political usage was metaphorical, describing a movement back into some pre-established point, and hence a motion, a swinging back to a pre-ordained order. The word was first used not when what we are apt to call a revolution broke out in England and Cromwell rose up as a sort of dictator, but on the contrary, in 1660, on the occasion of the re-establishment of the monarchy, after the overthrow of the Rump Parliament. But even the Glorious Revolution, the event through which, rather paradoxically, the term found its place in historical-political language, was not thought of as a revolution but as the restoration of monarchical power to its former righteousness and glory. The actual meaning of revolution, prior to the events of the late eighteenth century, is perhaps most clearly indicated in the inscription on the Great Seal of England of 1651, according to which the first transformation of monarchy into a republic meant: '*Freedom* by God's blessing *restored*'.

The fact that the word revolution originally meant restoration is more than a mere oddity of semantics. Even the eighteenth-century revolutions cannot be understood without realizing that revolutions first broke out when restoration had been their aim, and that the content of such restoration was freedom. In America, in the words of John Adams, the men of the revolution had been 'called without expectation and compelled without previous inclination'; the same is true for France where, in Tocqueville's words, 'one might have believed the aim of the coming revolution was the restoration of the *ancien régime* rather than its overthrow.' And in the course of both revolutions, when the actors became aware that they were embarking upon an entirely new enterprise rather than revolving back to anything preceding it, when the word 'revolution' consequently was acquiring its new meaning, it was Thomas Paine, of all people, who, still true to the spirit of the bygone age, proposed in all seriousness to call the American and French revolutions 'counter-revolutions'. He wanted to save the extraordinary events from the suspicion that an entirely new beginning had been made, and from the odium of violence with which these events were inevitably linked.

We are likely to overlook the almost instinctive horror manifest in the mentality of these first revolutionists before the entirely new. In part this is because we are so well acquainted with the eagerness of scientists and philosophers of the Modern Age for 'things never seen before and thoughts never thought before'.

And in part it is because nothing in the course of these revolutions is as conspicuous and striking as the emphatic stress on novelty, repeated over and over by actors and spectators alike, in their insistence that nothing comparable in significance and grandeur had ever happened before. The crucial and difficult point is that the enormous pathos of the new era, the *novus ordo seclorum*, which is still inscribed on our dollar bills, came to the fore only after the actors, much against their will, had reached a point of no return.

Hence, what actually happened at the end of the eighteenth century was that an attempt at restoration and recovery of old rights and privileges resulted in its exact opposite: a progressing development and the opening up of a future which defied all further attempts at acting or thinking in terms of a circular or revolving motion. And while the term 'revolution' was radically transformed in the revolutionary process, something similar, but infinitely more complex, happened to the word 'freedom'. As long as nothing more was meant by it than freedom 'by God's blessing *restored*', it remained a matter of those rights and liberties we today associate with constitutional government, which properly are called civil rights. What was not included in them was the political right to participate in public affairs. None of those other rights, including the right to be represented for purposes of taxation, were either in theory or practice the result of revolution. Not 'life, liberty, and property', but the claim that they were inalienable rights of all human creatures, no matter where they lived or what kind of government they enjoyed, was revolutionary. And even in this new and revolutionary extension to all mankind, liberty meant no more than freedom from unjustifiable restraint, that is, something essentially negative. Liberties in the sense of civil rights are the results of liberation, but they are by no means the actual content of freedom, whose essence is admission to the public realm and participation in public affairs. Had the revolutions aimed only at the guarantee of civil rights, liberation from regimes that had overstepped their powers and infringed upon well-established rights would have been enough. And it is true that the revolutions of the eighteenth century began by claiming those old rights. The complexity comes when revolution is concerned with both liberation and freedom, and, since liberation is indeed a condition of freedom – though freedom is by no means a necessary result of liberation – it is difficult to see and say where the desire for liberation, to be free from oppression, ends, and the desire for freedom, to live a political life, begins. The point of the matter is that liberation from oppression could very well have been fulfilled under monarchical though not tyrannical government, whereas the freedom of a political way of life required a new, or rather rediscovered, form of government. It demanded the constitution of a republic. Nothing, indeed, is more clearly borne out by the facts than Jefferson's retrospective claim 'that the contests of that day were contests of principle between the advocates of republican and those of kingly government'. The equation of a republican government with freedom, and the conviction that monarchy is a criminal government fit for slaves – though it became commonplace almost as soon as the revolutions began – had been quite absent from the minds of the revolutionaries themselves. Still, though this was a new freedom they were aiming at, it would be hard to maintain they had no prior notion of it. On the contrary, it was a passion for this new political freedom, though not yet equated with a republican form of government, which inspired and prepared those to enact a revolution without fully knowing what they were doing.

No revolution, no matter how wide it opened its gates to the masses and the downtrodden – *les malheureux, les misérables, les damnés de la terre* as we know them from the grand rhetoric of the French Revolution – was ever started by them. And no revolution was ever the result of conspiracies, secret societies, or openly revolutionary parties. Speaking generally, no revolution is even possible where the authority of the body politic is intact, which, under modern conditions, means where the armed forces can be trusted to obey the civil authorities. Revolutions are not necessary but possible answers to the devolution of a regime, not the cause but the consequence of the downfall of political authority. Wherever these disintegrative processes have been allowed to develop unchecked, usually over a prolonged period, revolutions *may* occur under the condition that a sufficient number of the populace exists which is prepared for a regime's collapse and is willing to assume power. Revolutions always appear to succeed with amazing ease in their initial stages, and the reason is that those who supposedly 'make' revolutions do not 'seize power' but rather pick it up where it lies in the streets.

If the men of the American and French revolutions had anything in common prior to the events which were to determine their lives, shape their convictions, and eventually draw them apart, it was a passionate longing to participate in public affairs, and a no less passionate disgust with the hypocrisy and foolishness of 'good society' – to which must be added a restlessness and more or less outspoken contempt for the pettiness of merely private affairs. In the sense of the formation of this very special mentality, John Adams was entirely right when he said that 'the revolution was effected before the war commenced,' not because of a specifically revolutionary or rebellious spirit, but because the inhabitants of the colonies were 'formed by law into corporations, or bodies politic' with the 'right to assemble . . . in their own town halls, there to deliberate upon public affairs,' for it was indeed 'in these assemblies of towns or districts that the sentiments of the people were formed in the first place'. To be sure, nothing comparable to the political institutions in the colonies existed in France, but the mentality was still the same; what Tocqueville called a 'passion' and 'taste' in France was in America an experience manifest from the earliest times of colonization, in fact ever since the Mayflower Compact had been a veritable school of public spirit and public freedom. Prior to the revolutions, these men on both sides of the Atlantic were called *hommes de lettres*, and it is characteristic of them that they spent their leisure time 'ransacking the archives of antiquity', that is, turning to Roman history, not because they were romantically enamored of the past as such but with the purpose of recovering the spiritual as well as institutional political lessons that had been lost or half-forgotten during the centuries of a strictly Christian tradition. 'The world has been empty since the Romans, and is filled only with their memory, which is now our prophecy of freedom,' exclaimed Saint-Just, as before him Thomas Paine had predicted 'what Athens was in miniature, America will be in magnitude.'

To understand the role of antiquity in the history of revolutions we would have to recall the enthusiasm for 'ancient prudence' with which Harrington and Milton greeted Cromwell's dictatorship, and how this enthusiasm had been revived in the eighteenth century by Montesquieu's *Considerations on the*

Causes of the Grandeur and the Decadence of the Romans.
Without the classical example of what politics could
be and participation in public affairs could mean for
the happiness of man, none of the men of the revolutions would have possessed the courage for what
would appear as unprecedented action. Historically
speaking, it was as if the Renaissance's revival of
antiquity was suddenly granted a new lease on life,
as if the republican fervor of the short-lived Italian
city-states, foredoomed by the advent of the nation-
state, had only lain dormant, so to speak, to give the
nations of Europe the time to grow up under the
tutelage of absolute princes and enlightened despots.
The first elements of a political philosophy corresponding to this notion of public freedom are spelled
out in John Adam's writings. His point of departure
is the observation that 'Wherever men, women, or
children are to be found, whether they be old or young,
rich or poor, high or low . . . ignorant or learned,
every individual is seen to be strongly actuated by a
desire to be seen, heard, talked of, approved and
respected by the people about him and within his
knowledge.' The virtue of this 'desire' Adams saw
in 'the desire to excel another', and its vice he called
'ambition', which 'aims at power as a means of distinction'. And these two indeed are among the chief
virtues and vices of political man. For the will to

power as such, regardless of any passion for distinction (in which power is not a means but an end), is characteristic of the tyrant and is no longer even a political vice. It is rather the quality that tends to destroy all political life, its vices no less than its virtues. It is precisely because the tyrant has no desire to excel and lacks all passion for distinction that he finds it so pleasant to dominate, thereby excluding himself from the company of others; conversely, it is the desire to excel which makes men love the company of their peers and spurs them on into the public realm. This public freedom is a tangible worldly reality, created by men to enjoy together in public – to be seen, heard, known, and remembered by others. And this kind of freedom demands equality, it is possible only amongst peers. Institutionally speaking, it is possible only in a republic, which knows no subjects and, strictly speaking, no rulers. This is the reason why discussions of the forms of government, in sharp contrast to later ideologies, played such an enormous role in the thinking and writing of the first revolutionaries.

No doubt, it is obvious and of great consequence that this passion for freedom for its own sake awoke in and was nourished by men of leisure, by the *hommes de lettres* who had no masters and were not always busy making a living. In other words, they enjoyed the privileges of Athenian and Roman citizens without taking part in those affairs of state that so occupied the free-men of antiquity. Needless to add, where men live in truly miserable conditions this passion for freedom is unknown. And if we need additional proof of the absence of such conditions in the colonies, the 'lovely equality' in America where, as Jefferson put it, 'the most conspicuously wretched individual' was better off than nineteen out of the twenty million inhabitants of France, we need only remember that John Adams ascribed this love of freedom to 'poor and rich, high and low, ignorant and learned'. It is the chief, perhaps the only reason, why the principles that inspired the men of the first revolutions were triumphantly victorious in America and failed tragically in France. Seen with American eyes, a republican government in France was 'as unnatural, irrational, and impracticable as it would be over elephants, lions, tigers, panthers, wolves, and bears in the royal menagerie at Versailles' (John Adams). The reason why the attempt was made nevertheless is that those who made it, *les hommes de lettres*, were not much different from their American colleagues; it was only in the course of the French Revolution that they learned they were acting under radically different circumstances.

The circumstances differed in political as well as

social respects. Even the rule of King and Parliament in England was 'mild government' in comparison with French absolutism. Under its auspices, England developed an intricate and well-functioning regime of self-government, which needed only the explicit foundation of a republic to confirm its existence. Still, these political differences, though important enough, were negligible compared with the formidable obstacle to the constitution of freedom inherent in the social conditions of Europe. The men of the first revolutions, though they knew well enough that liberation had to precede freedom, were still unaware of the fact that such liberation means more than political liberation from absolute and despotic power; that to be free for freedom meant first of all to be free not only from fear but also from want. And the condition of desperate poverty of the masses of the people, those who for the first time burst into the open when they streamed into the streets of Paris, could not be overcome with political means; the mighty power of the constraint under which they labored did not crumble before the onslaught of the revolution as did the royal power of the king. The American Revolution was fortunate that it did not have to face this obstacle to freedom and, in fact, owed a good measure of its success to the absence of desperate poverty among the free-men, and to the invisibility of slaves, in the colonies of the New World. To be sure, there was poverty and misery in America, which was comparable to the conditions of the European 'laboring poor'. If, in William Penn's words, 'America was a good poor Man's country' and remained the dream of a promised land for Europe's impoverished up to the beginning of the twentieth century, it is no less true that this goodness depended to a considerable degree on black misery. In the middle of the eighteenth century, there lived roughly 400,000 blacks along with approximately 1,850,00 whites in America, and, despite the absence of reliable statistical information, it may be doubted that at the time the percentage of complete destitution was higher in the countries of the Old World (though it would become considerably higher during the nineteenth century). The difference, then, was that the American Revolution – because of the institution of slavery and the belief that slaves belonged to a different 'race' – overlooked the existence of the miserable, and with it the formidable task of liberating those who were not so much constrained by political oppression as the sheer necessities of life. *Les malheureux*, the wretched, who play such a tremendous role in the course of the French Revolution, which identified them with *le peuple*, either did not exist or remained in complete obscurity in America.

One of the principal consequences of the revolution in France was, for the first time in history, to bring *le peuple* into the streets and make them visible. When this happened it turned out that not just freedom but the freedom to be free had always been the privilege of the few. By the same token, however, the American Revolution has remained without much consequence for the historical understanding of revolutions, while the French Revolution, which ended in resounding failure, has determined and is still determining what now we call the revolutionary tradition.

What then happened in Paris in 1789? First, freedom from fear is a privilege that even the few have enjoyed in only relatively short periods of history, but freedom from want has been the great privilege that has distinguished a very small percentage of mankind throughout the centuries. What we tend to call the recorded history of mankind is, for the most part, the history of those privileged few. Only those who know freedom from want can appreciate fully the meaning of freedom from fear, and only those who are free from both want and fear are in a position to conceive a passion for public freedom, to develop within themselves that *goût* or taste for *liberté* and the peculiar taste for *égalité* or equality that *liberté* carries within it.

Speaking schematically, it may be said that each revolution goes first through the stage of liberation before it can attain to freedom, the second and decisive stage of the foundation of a new form of government and a new body politic. In the course of the American Revolution, the stage of liberation meant liberation from political restraint, from tyranny or monarchy or whatever word may have been used. The first stage was characterized by violence, but the second stage was a matter of deliberation, discussion, and persuasion, in short, of applying 'political science' as the Founders understood the term. But in France something altogether different happened. The first stage of the revolution is much better characterized by disintegration rather than by violence, and when the second stage was reached and the National Convention had declared France to be a republic, power already had shifted to the streets. The men who had gathered in Paris to represent *la nation* rather than *le peuple*, whose chief concern – whether their name was Mirabeau or Robespierre, Danton or Saint-Just – had been government, the reformation of monarchy, and later the foundation of a republic, saw themselves suddenly confronted with yet another task of liberation, that is, liberating the people at large from wretchedness: to free them to be free. This was not yet what both Marx and Tocqueville would see as the entirely new feature of the revolution of 1848, the switch from changing the form of government to the attempt to alter the order of society by means of class struggle. Only after February 1848, after 'the first great battle . . . between the two classes that split society,' Marx noted that revolution now meant 'the overthrow of bourgeois society, whereas before it had meant the overthrow of the form of state'. The French Revolution of 1789 was the prelude to this, and though it ended in dismal failure, it remained decisive for all later revolutions. It showed what the new formula, namely, all men are created equal, meant in practice. And it was this equality that Robespierre had in mind when he said that revolution pits the grandeur of man against the pettiness of the great; and Hamilton as well, when he spoke of the revolution having vindicated the honor of the human race; and also Kant, taught by Rousseau and the French Revolution, when he conceived of a new dignity of man. Whatever the French Revolution did and did not achieve – and it did not achieve human equality – it liberated the poor from obscurity, from nonvisibility. What has seemed irrevocable ever since is that those who were devoted to freedom could remain reconciled to a state of affairs in which freedom from want – *the freedom to be free* – was a privilege of the few.

Apropos of the original constellation of the

revolutionaries and the masses of the poor they happened to bring into the open, let me quote Lord Acton's interpretive description of the women's march to Versailles, among the most prominent turning points of the French Revolution. The marchers, he said, 'played the genuine part of mothers whose children were starving in squalid homes, and they thereby afforded to motives, which they neither shared nor understood [i.e., concern with government] the aid of a diamond point that nothing could withstand.' What *le peuple*, as the French understood it, brought to the revolution and which was altogether absent from the course of events in America, was the irresistibility of a movement that human power was no longer able to control. This elementary experience of irresistibility – as irresistible as the motions of stars – brought forth an entirely new imagery, which still today we almost automatically associate in our thoughts of revolutionary events. When Saint-Just exclaimed, under the impact of what he saw before his eyes, *'Les malheureux sont la puissance de la terre,'* he meant the great 'revolutionary torrent' (Desmoulins) on whose rushing waves the actors were borne and carried away until its undertow sucked them from the surface and they perished together with their foes, the agents of counter-revolution. Or Robespierre's tempest and mighty current, which was nourished by the crimes of tyranny on one side and by the progress of liberty on the other, constantly increased in rapidity and violence. Or what the spectators reported – a 'majestic lava stream which spares nothing and which nobody can arrest', a spectacle that had fallen under the sign of Saturn, 'the revolution devouring its own children' (Vergniaud). The words I am quoting here were all spoken by men deeply involved in the French Revolution and testify to things witnessed by them, that is, not to things they had done or set out to do intentionally. This is what happened, and it taught men a lesson that in neither hope nor fear has ever been forgotten. The lesson, as simple as it was new and unexpected, is, as Saint-Just put it, 'If you wish to found a republic, you first must pull the people out of a condition of misery that corrupts them. There are no political virtues without pride, and no one can have pride who is wretched.'

This new notion of freedom, resting upon liberation from poverty, changed both the course and goal of revolution. Liberty now had come to mean first of all 'dress and food and the reproduction of the species,' as the *sans-culottes* consciously distinguished their own rights from the lofty and, to them, meaningless language of the proclamation of the Rights of Man and of the Citizen. Compared to the urgency of their demands, all deliberations about the best form of government suddenly appeared irrelevant and futile. '*La République? La Monarchie? Je ne connais que la question sociale,*' said Robespierre. And Saint-Just, who had started out with the greatest possible enthusiasm for 'republican institutions', would add, 'The freedom of the people is in its private life. Let government be only the force to protect this state of simplicity against force itself.' He might not have known it, but that was precisely the credo of enlightened despots which held, with Charles I of England in his speech from the scaffold, that the people's 'liberty and freedom consists in having the government of those laws by which their life and their goods may be most their own; 'tis not for having share in Government, that is nothing pertaining to them.' If it were true, as all participants moved by the misery of the people suddenly agreed, that the goal of revolutions was the happiness of the people – *le but de la Révolution est le bonheur du peuple* – then it indeed could be provided by a sufficiently enlightened despotic government rather than a republic.

The French Revolution ended in disaster and became a turning point in world history; the American Revolution was a triumphant success and remained a local affair, partly of course because social conditions in the world at large were far more similar to those in France, and partly because the much praised Anglo-Saxon pragmatic tradition prevented subsequent generations of Americans from *thinking* about their revolution and adequately conceptualizing its experience. It is therefore not surprising that the despotism, or actually the return to the age of enlightened absolutism, which announced itself clearly in the course of the French Revolution, became the rule for almost all subsequent revolutions, or at least those that did not end in restoration of the *status quo ante*, and even became dominant in revolutionary theory. I don't need to follow this development in detail; it is sufficiently well known, especially from the history of the Bolshevik party and the Russian Revolution. Moreover, it was predictable: in the late summer of 1918 – after the promulgation of the Soviet constitution but prior to the first wave of terror prompted by the attempted assassination of Lenin – Rosa Luxemburg, in a private, later published, and now famous letter, wrote as follows:

> With the repression of political life in the land as a whole . . . life dies out in every public institution, becoming a mere semblance of life, in which only the bureaucracy remains as

the active element. Public life gradually falls asleep. The few dozen party leaders of inexhaustible energy and boundless experience direct and rule. Among them only a dozen outstanding heads do the ruling, and an elite of the working class is invited from time to time to meetings where its members are to applaud the speeches of the leaders, and to approve proposed resolutions unanimously . . . A dictatorship, to be sure; not the dictatorship of the proletariat, however, but of a handful of politicians.

That this is how it turned out – except for Stalin's totalitarian rule, for which it would be difficult to hold either Lenin or the revolutionary tradition responsible – no one is likely to deny. But what is perhaps less obvious is that one would have to change only a few words to obtain a perfect description of the ills of absolutism prior to the revolutions.

A comparison of the two first revolutions, whose beginnings were so similar and whose ends so tremendously different, demonstrates clearly, I think, not only that the conquest of poverty is a prerequisite for the foundation of freedom, but also that liberation from poverty cannot be dealt with in the same way as liberation from political oppression.

For if violence pitted against violence leads to war, foreign or civil, violence pitted against social conditions has always led to terror. Terror rather than mere violence, terror let loose after the old regime has been dissolved and the new regime installed, is what either sends revolutions to their doom, or deforms them so decisively that they lapse into tyranny and despotism.

I said before that the revolution's original goal was freedom in the sense of the abolition of personal rule and of the admission of all to public realm and participation in the administration of affairs common to all. Rulership itself had its most legitimate source not in a drive to power but in the human wish to emancipate mankind from the necessities of life, the achievement of which required violence, the means of forcing the many to bear the burdens of the few so that at least some could be free. This, and not the accumulation of wealth, was the core of slavery, at least in antiquity, and it is due only to the rise of modern technology, rather than the rise of any modern political notions, including revolutionary ideas, which has changed this human condition at least in some parts of the world. What America achieved by great good luck, today many other states, though probably not all, may acquire by virtue of calculated effort and organized development.

This fact is the measure of our hope. It permits us to take the lessons of the deformed revolutions into account and still hold fast not only to their undeniable grandeur but also to their inherent promise.

Let me, by way of concluding, just indicate one more aspect of freedom which came to the fore during the revolutions, and for which the revolutionaries themselves were least prepared. It is that the idea of freedom and the actual experience of making a new beginning in the historical continuum should coincide. Let me remind you once more of the *Novus Ordo Saeclorum*. The surprising phrase is based on Virgil, who, in his Fourth *Eclogue*, speaks of 'the great cycle of periods [that] is born anew' in the reign of Augustus: *Magnus ab integro saeclorum nascitur ordo*. Virgil speaks of a *great* (*magnus*) but not a *new* (*novus*) order, and it is this change in a line much quoted throughout the centuries that is characteristic of the experiences of the modern age. For Virgil – now in the language of the seventeenth century – it was a question of founding Rome 'anew', but not of founding a 'new Rome'. This way he escaped, in typically Roman fashion, the fearful risks of violence inherent in breaking the tradition of Rome, i.e., the handed-down (*traditio*) story of the founding of the eternal city by suggesting a new beginning. Now, of course we could argue that the new beginning, which the spectators of the first revolutions thought they were watching, was only the rebirth of something quite old: the renascence of a secular political realm finally arising from Christianity, feudalism, and absolutism. But no matter whether it is a question of birth or rebirth, what is decisive in Virgil's line is that it is taken from a nativity hymn, not prophesying the birth of a divine child, but in praise of *birth as such*, the arrival of a new generation, the great saving event or 'miracle' which will redeem mankind time and again. In other words, it is the affirmation of the divinity of birth, and the belief that the world's potential salvation lies in the very fact that the human species regenerates itself constantly and forever.

What made the men of the revolution go back to this particular poem of antiquity, quite apart from their erudition, I would suggest, was not only that the pre-revolutionary *idea* of freedom but also the experience of being free coincided, or rather was intimately interwoven, with beginning something new, with metaphorically speaking, the birth of a new era. To be free and to start something new were felt to be the same. And obviously, this mysterious human gift, the ability to start something new, is connected to the fact that every one of us came into the world as a newcomer through birth. In other words, we can begin something because we *are* beginnings and hence beginners. Insofar as the capacity for acting and speaking – and speaking is but another mode of acting – makes us political beings, and since acting always has meant to set in motion what was not there before, birth or human natality, which corresponds to human mortality, is the ontological condition *sine qua non* of all politics. This was known in both Greek and Roman antiquity, albeit in an inexplicit manner. It came to the fore in the experiences of revolution, and it has influenced, though again rather inexplicitly, what one may call the revolutionary spirit. At any rate, the chain of revolutions, which for better and worse has become the hallmark of the world we live in, time after time discloses to us the eruption of new beginnings within the temporal and historical continuum. For us, who owe it to a revolution and the resulting foundation of an entirely new body politic that we can walk in dignity and act in freedom, it would be wise to remember what a revolution means in the life of nations. Whether it ends in success, with the constitution of a public space for freedom, or in disaster, for those who have risked it or participated in it against their inclination and expectation, the meaning of revolution is the actualization of one of the greatest and most elementary human potentialities, the unequaled experience of *being* free to make a new beginning, from which comes the pride of having opened the world to a *Novus Ordo Saeclorum*.

To sum up: Niccolò Machiavelli, whom one may well call the 'father of revolutions', most passionately desired a new order of things for Italy, yet could hardly yet speak with any great amount of experience of these matters. Thus he still believed that the 'innovators', i.e., the revolutionists, would encounter their greatest difficulty in the beginning when taking power, and find retaining it far easier. We know from practically all revolutions that the opposite is the case – that it is relatively easy to seize power but infinitely more difficult to keep it – as Lenin, no bad witness in such matters, once remarked. Still, Machiavelli knew enough to say the following: 'There is nothing more difficult to carry out, nor more doubtful of success, nor more dangerous to handle, than to initiate a new order of things.' With this sentence, I suppose, no one who understands anything at all of the story of the twentieth century will quarrel. Moreover, the dangers Machiavelli expected to arise have proved to be quite real up to our own day, despite the fact that he was not yet aware of the greatest danger in modern revolutions – the danger that rises from poverty. He mentions what since the French Revolution have been called counter-revolutionary forces, represented by those 'who profit from the old order', and the 'luke-warmness' of those who might profit from the new order because of 'the incredulity of mankind, of those who do not truly believe in any new thing until they have experienced it'. However, the point of the matter is that Machiavelli saw the danger only in defeat of the attempt to found a new order of things, that is, in the sheer weakening of the country in which the attempt is made. This too has proved to be the case, for such weakness, i.e., the power vacuum of which I spoke before, may well attract conquerors. Not that this power vacuum did not previously exist, but it can remain hidden for years until some decisive event happens, when the collapse of authority and a revolution make it manifest in dramatic calls into the open where it can be seen and known by all. In addition to all this, we have witnessed the supreme danger that out of the abortive attempt to found the institutions of freedom may grow the most thoroughgoing abolition of freedom and of all liberties.

Precisely because revolutions put the question of political freedom in its truest and most radical form – freedom to participate in public affairs, freedom of action – all other freedoms, political as well as civil liberties, are in jeopardy when revolutions fail. Deformed revolutions, such as the October Revolution in Russia under Lenin, or abortive revolutions, such as the various upheavals among the European central powers after World War I, may have, as we now know, consequences which in sheer horror are well-nigh unprecedented. The point of the matter is that revolutions rarely are reversible, that once they have happened they are not forgettable – as Kant remarked about the French Revolution at a time when terror ruled in France. This cannot possibly mean that therefore the best is to prevent revolutions, for if revolutions are the consequences of regimes in full disintegration, and not the 'product' of revolutionaries – be they organized in conspiratorial sects or in parties – then to prevent a revolution means to change the form of government, which itself means to effect a revolution with all the dangers and hazards that entails. The collapse of authority and power, which as a rule comes with surprising suddenness not only to the readers of newspapers but also to all secret services and their experts who watch such things, becomes a revolution in the full sense of the word only when there are people willing and capable of picking up the power, of moving into and penetrating, so to speak, the power vacuum. What then happens depends upon many circumstances, not least upon the degree of insight of foreign powers into the irreversibility of revolutionary practices. But it depends most of all upon subjective qualities and the moral-political success or failure of those who are willing to assume responsibility. We have little reason to hope that at some time in the not-too-distant future such men will match in practical and theoretical wisdom the men of the American Revolution, who became the Founders of this country. But that little hope, I fear, is the only one we have that freedom in a political sense will not vanish again from the earth for God knows how many centuries.

1966–1967